Pete Cassidy's
Cookbook
For Oracle SQL*Plus™

Pete Cassidy's Cookbook For Oracle SQL*Plus

Published by Chef Pierre

ISBN: 0-9656696-0-2

Printed in USA.

.
Print Date: 16-OCT-95
Version Date: 01-FEB-2000

ORACLE, CASE Dictionary, CASE Designer, PRO*Ada, PRO*Cobol, PRO*C, PRO*Fortran, PRO*Pascal, PRO*Pl/1, SQL*Forms, SQL*Plus, SQL*Report, SQL*ReportWriter, Oracle Forms, Oracle Reports, and Oracle Graphics are registered trademarks of the Oracle Corporation. ORACLE7, Cooperative Development Environment, CASE Generator, CASE Exchange, Oracle CASE, Oracle Parallel Server are trademarks of the Oracle Corporation. CASE Method is a service mark of the Oracle Corporation.

Publisher
Chef Pierre

Author
Pete Cassidy

Editor
Carole Cassidy

Cover Design
Carole Cassidy

Photography
Debra Kay Cassidy
French Titles
Paige Larue Cassidy

Contents

Acknowledgments

To my wife, Carole, for all of her patience and creativity.

For my children – Debra and Paige.

If a man asks you to walk one mile, walk three; anything worth doing is worth doing well; you shall seek the truth, and the truth shall set you free.

Foreword

For years students have been asking me "What is one book that simplifies how to use Oracle ?" I did not have an adequate answer for them. So, I tried my best to give examples and little cheat sheet helps of my own. My handouts were so well received that students began to urge me to make them available in book form; this cookbook is my first attempt to meet that need. The most urgent demand seemed to be SQL*Plus. Therefore, it is the FIRST of my cookbook series. I plan to make available cookbooks using the same format for:

Oracle8I SQL Statement Tuning.

The purpose of this cookbook series is to answer the question of, "What should I see on the terminal, and if something goes wrong, how can I fix it?" This is not one of those wordy volumes that go off on tangents of all the different possibilities; but rather, it is an example of the more common solutions to the problems most frequently encountered in Oracle.

This is called a COOKBOOK because just as in a kitchen cookbook, one finds a step by step process of how to successfully prepare a recipe without an explanation of why each step is completed; this book gives a step-by-step recipe for success in Oracle without much discussion. Like Sergeant Friday said, "Just the facts Ma'am."

The recipes were created by Chef Pierre. The nickname, Chef Pierre, was "cooked" up by my family, because for years I have talked about getting this cookbook together like I was a big Chef of Oracle. This is when I have to confess that my real name is Pierre Cassidy. You've known me as Pete, and I worked hard to keep the Pierre from you, since the seventh grade when I got fed up with the name "Pee-In-The-Air". Isn't it odd that after all the years running from the name Pierre, that I have become the Chef Pierre of Oracle Cookbooks? What else can I say: **"use them and Bon Appe′tit."**

Pete Cassidy

Preface

Just as a cookbook does not teach one how to cook, but gives one the instructions to implement his/her knowledge, Pete Cassidy's Cookbooks give the information to implement the use of Oracle. This cookbook is not meant to teach Oracle; it is assumed the user already possesses a working knowledge of the Oracle software.
It is not my intention to say this book contains the only way to get the job done. These recipes are the result of what I have found to be successful in my eight years of working with the Oracle products. Just as a kitchen cookbook contains a version of a recipe, this cookbook contains only Pete Cassidy's recipes for Oracle; although, I'm sure many other methods exist.

Many of the examples were formatted with the "COLUMN" command, and most are not included. In other instances, the "SUBSTR" function was used for formatting purposes.

With respect to the DATA DICTIONARY, examples are against "USER_" and "DBA_" depending upon the MOOD of the author.

As far as we know, all jokes are ANONYMOUS. The ones I use are so bad anyway, I don't think anyone would have nerve enough to claim them!

This book was written on various and sundry machines, and releases of Oracle software. However, everything was performed using Oracle 7, and mostly on a SUN.

The reader will observe many get cb999 commands. These are files written by the author to expedite the writing of this document. Therefore, if you try the same on your platform, you will NOT FIND those script files.

The author also had to get very creative with some of the "WHERE" clauses, to limit the size of the output, so everything would fit on a page.

Chief Pierre does not guarantee the accuracy, adequacy, or completeness of any information, and is not responsible for any errors or omissions or the results obtained from the use of such information, since there always remains the possibility of human or mechanical errors.

> All commands actually entered are in **BOLD**, and the terminal output is *ITALICS*.
> Relevant information on the terminal is in ***BOLD ITALICS.***

CHAPTER

1

Breakfast (Petit De'jeuner)
Or
Getting Started

Determining Your Home And SID On Unix Boxes

```
> env | grep ora
PATH=.:/home2/dci2/pcassidy/bin:/usr/5bin:/bin:/usr/ucb:/usr
/bin:/usr/kvm:/usr/openwin/bin:/usr/bin/X11:/etc:/usr/etc:/u
sr/lang:/home2/oracle/7.1.3/bin:/usr/local/bin
ORACLE_HOME=/home2/oracle/7.1.3
ORACLE_SID=ora713
ORATERMPATH=.:/home2/oracle/7.1.3/forms30/admin/resource
MENU5PATH=.:/home2/oracle/7.1.3/forms30/admin/resource
FORMS30PATH=.:/home2/oracle/7.1.3/forms30/admin/resource
ORAKITPATH=.:/home2/oracle/7.1.3/forms30/admin/resource
ORACLE_PATH=.:/home2/dci2/pcassidy/dba/sql:/home2/oracle/7.1
.3/rdbms/admin
APIPATH=/home2/oracle/7.1.3/rdbms/admin/resource
```

Your Oracle *System Identifier* is ora7.1.3, and your Oracle *home directory* is /home2/oracle/7.1.3. Also note your *PATH*.

Determining Which Release You Are Executing

Method 1:

```
> sqlplus student15/student15

SQL*Plus: Release 3.1.3.4.1 - Production on Tue Aug 15
18:21:06 1995

Copyright (c) Oracle Corporation 1979, 1994.  All rights
reserved.

Connected to:
Oracle7 Server Release 7.1.3.0.0 - Production Release
With the distributed and parallel query options
PL/SQL Release 2.1.3.0.0 - Production
```

Method 2:

```
SQL> DEF
DEFINE _EDITOR          = "vi " (CHAR)
DEFINE _O_VERSION       = "Oracle7 Server Release 7.1.3.0.0 -
Production Release
With the distributed and parallel query options
PL/SQL Release 2.1.3.0.0 - Production" (CHAR)
DEFINE _O_RELEASE       = "701030000" (CHAR)
```

Method 3:

```
SQL> get cb361
  1  SELECT *
  2* FROM    V$VERSION
SQL> /

BANNER
----------------------------------------------------------
Oracle7 Server Release 7.1.3.0.0 - Production Release
PL/SQL Release 2.1.3.0.0 - Production
CORE Version 2.3.3.4.0 - Production (LSF Alpha)
TNS for SunOS: Version 2.1.3.0.0 - Production
NLSRTL Version 2.3.4.2.1 - Production
```

Determining Which Database You Are Using

```
SQL> SELECT *
  2  FROM    V$DATABASE;
```

NAME	CREATED	LOG_MODE	CHECKPOINT _CHANGE#	ARCHIVE _CHANGE#
ORA713	12/27/94 14:56:27	NOARCHIVELOG	279496	279186

Determining Which Options Are In Your Database

```
SQL> DESC V$OPTION
 Name                                    Null?    Type
 -------------------------------- -------- ----
 PARAMETER                                         VARCHAR2(64)
 VALUE                                             VARCHAR2(64)




SQL> COL PARAMETER FORMAT A15
SQL> COL VALUE      FORMAT A5




SQL> SELECT *
  2  FROM    V$OPTION
  3  ORDER  BY PARAMETER;




PARAMETER       VALUE
--------------- -----
Parallel Server FALSE
distributed     TRUE
parallel query  TRUE
procedural      TRUE
```

Determining How Many Data Dictionary Views Exist

```
SQL> SELECT COUNT(*)
  2  FROM    DICTIONARY;

  COUNT(*)
----------
       262



SQL> SELECT COUNT(*)   -- Dict Is A Public Synonym
  2  FROM    DICT;

  COUNT(*)
----------
       262
```

```
This number is constantly increasing as Oracle releases new
versions of their software.
```

Determining Data Dictionary Views By Subject

```
SQL> SELECT  TABLE_NAME
  2  FROM    DICT                    /*  Or Dictionary  */
  3  WHERE   TABLE_NAME LIKE '%' || UPPER('&Subject') || '%';

Enter value for subject: InD

TABLE_NAME
------------------------------
ALL_INDEXES
ALL_IND_COLUMNS
DBA_INDEXES
DBA_IND_COLUMNS
USER_INDEXES
USER_IND_COLUMNS
INDEX_HISTOGRAM
INDEX_STATS
IND

9 rows selected.
```

DBA_IND_COLUMNS, ALL_IND_COLUMNS, and USER_IND_COLUMNS
contain information about concatenated indexes.

Mr. String tried to get a drink at the bar yesterday, and the bartender said, "We don't serve STRINGS !!!". So, Mr. String went outside, where it was very windy, and got all tangled up, and returned and said, "Mr. Bartender, give me my drink !". The bartender then shouted, "I told you we don't serve STRINGS !!". And, Mr. String replied, "You don't understand,
* * * * * * *   PUNCH LINE COMING UP   * * * * * * *
I am a FRAYED KNOT !!!".

Determining Oracle User Name

Method 1:

```
SQL> SHOW USER
user is "STUDENT15"'
```

Method 2:

```
SQL> SELECT USER
  2  FROM   DUAL;


USER
------------------------------
STUDENT15
```

Many years ago, I had a student named Hadacall Johnson. One day curiosity got the better of me, so I asked him how in the world he received such an unusual name. He replied, "I have 17 brothers, and 12 sisters, and they ran out of names, and they HADACALL me something!".

Determining Your Assigned Role(s)

```
SQL> COL USERNAME      FORMAT A9
SQL> COL GRANTED_ROLE  FORMAT A15
SQL> COL ADMIN_OPTION  FORMAT A12
SQL> COL DEFAULT_ROLE  FORMAT A12
SQL> COL OS_GRANTED    FORMAT A10



SQL> SELECT *
  2  FROM   USER_ROLE_PRIVS;



USERNAME   GRANTED_ROLE  ADMIN_OPTION DEFAULT_ROLE OS_GRANTED
---------  ------------- ------------ ------------ ----------
STUDENT15  STUD          NO           YES          NO
```

> *Kind of reminds me of an old song about a Tennessee STUD.*

Determining Your Default Role

```
SQL> COL     GRANTEE        FORMAT A14
SQL> COL     GRANTED_ROLE   FORMAT A13
SQL> BREAK ON GRANTEE       SKIP 1



SQL> SELECT  GRANTEE,
  2          GRANTED_ROLE,
  3          DEFAULT_ROLE
  4   FROM   SYS.DBA_ROLE_PRIVS /*   Must Have DBA Priv  */
  5   WHERE  DEFAULT_ROLE = 'YES' AND
  6          GRANTEE IN('LARRY', 'CURLY', 'MOE')
  7   ORDER  BY GRANTEE;
```

GRANTEE	GRANTED_ROLE	DEFAULT_ROLE
HARRY	TWEE_STOOPES	YES
BURLY	TWEE_STOOPES	YES
JOE	TWEE_STOOPES	YES

Determining Which Commands Are Permissable In A Role

```
SQL> SET    VERIFY     OFF
SQL> BREAK ON          ROLE
SQL> COL    ROLE       FORMAT    A19
SQL> COL    PRIVILEGE  FORMAT    A27



SQL> SELECT *
  2  FROM    SYS.ROLE_SYS_PRIVS
  3  WHERE   ROLE LIKE '%' || UPPER('&Role') || '%';

Enter value for role: St


ROLE                  PRIVILEGE                    ADMIN_OPTION
-------------------   ---------------------------  ------------
STUD                  ALTER SESSION                NO
                      CREATE CLUSTER               NO
                      CREATE PROCEDURE             NO
                      CREATE SEQUENCE              NO
                      CREATE SESSION               NO
                      CREATE SYNONYM               NO
                      CREATE TABLE                 NO
                      CREATE TRIGGER               NO
                      CREATE VIEW                  NO
                      SELECT ANY TABLE             NO


10 rows selected.
```

Determining Your Default Tablespace

```
SQL> COL USERNAME             FORMAT A10
SQL> COL DEFAULT_TABLESPACE    FORMAT A19
SQL> COL TEMPORARY_TABLESPACE FORMAT A20




SQL> SELECT USERNAME,
  2         DEFAULT_TABLESPACE,
  3         TEMPORARY_TABLESPACE
  4  FROM    SYS.DBA_USERS
  5  WHERE   USERNAME = 'STUDENT15'
  6
SQL> /




USERNAME   DEFAULT_TABLESPACE   TEMPORARY_TABLESPACE
---------- -------------------- --------------------
STUDENT15  USER_DATA            TEMP
```

Determining Which Application Tables You Can Use

```
SQL> SHOW USER
user is "STUDENT15"

SQL> CREATE TABLE DRIVERS
  2          (DNO     NUMBER(3),
  3           DNAME   VARCHAR2(20));
Table created.
SQL> INSERT INTO DRIVERS VALUES(1, 'BILLY VUKIVICH');
1 row created.

SQL> GRANT SELECT ON DRIVERS TO STUDENT1;
Grant succeeded.

SQL> get cb16
  1   UNDEFINE GRANTEE
  2   COL     "Tables"   FORMAT   A25
  3   SELECT GRANTOR || '.' || TABLE_NAME "Tables"
  4   FROM    SYS.DBA_TAB_PRIVS
  5   WHERE   GRANTEE = UPPER('&&GRANTEE')
  6   UNION
  7   SELECT TABLE_NAME
  8   FROM    SYS.DBA_TABLES
  9   WHERE   OWNER = UPPER('&GRANTEE')
 10*  ORDER   BY 1

SQL> @cb16
Enter value for grantee: StUdENT1

Tables
-------------------------
DEPT
EMP
STUDENT15.DRIVERS
```

Identifying The Primary Keys For A Table

```
SQL> get cb18
  1   COL    COLUMN_NAME                    FORMAT        A15
  2   COL    CONSTRAINT_NAME                FORMAT        A16
  3   SELECT A.TABLE_NAME,
  4          A.COLUMN_NAME,
  5          A.CONSTRAINT_NAME,
  6          A.POSITION,
  7          B.STATUS
  8   FROM   SYS.DBA_CONS_COLUMNS A,
  9          SYS.DBA_CONSTRAINTS B
 10   WHERE  A.TABLE_NAME        =      B.TABLE_NAME    AND
 11          B.CONSTRAINT_TYPE   =      'P'             AND
 12          A.OWNER             =      UPPER('&Owner') AND
 13          A.TABLE_NAME        =      UPPER('&Table')
 14*  ORDER  BY                         A.POSITION
SQL>


SQL> @cb18
Enter value for owner: StUdeNT15
Enter value for table: drivERS



TABLE_NAME COLUMN_NAME CONSTRAINT_NAME POSITION STATUS
---------- ----------- --------------- -------- -------
DRIVERS    DNO         PK_DRIVERS_DNO         1 ENABLED
```

What It Looks Like When Oracle Is Shut Down

```
> sqlplus student15/student15
```

SQL*Plus: Release 3.1.3.2.1 - Production on Wed Mar 29 12:12:26 1995

Copyright (c) Oracle Corporation 1979, 1992. All rights reserved.

ERROR: ORA-01034: ORACLE not available
ORA-07429: smsgsg: shmget() failed to get segment.
SunOS Error: 2: No such file or directory

Enter user-name: **^C**

```
> oerr ora 1034
```
01034, 00000, "ORACLE not available"
// *Cause:
// *Action:

```
Sometimes the above operating system command is quite
helpful.  This is one time it is not.  At least you
do not have to try and locate the Oracle Error and Messages
manual, which is almost impossible.  And, if you do find it
you don't have to lug it around with you, and look up
messages.
```

What Happens After A Shutdown "Immediate"

```
SQL> SELECT *
     FROM    EMP;
SELECT *
FROM    EMP
ERROR at line 1:
ORA-03113: end-of-file on communication channel



SQL> DESC EMP
ERROR:
ORA-03114: not connected to Oracle
```

After Oracle Is Re-Started

```
SQL> CONNECT STUDENT15/STUDENT15
Connected.
```

Determining Which Files Are In Your Database

```
SQL> SELECT SUBSTR(NAME, 1, 70) "Name"    FROM V$DATAFILE
  2  UNION
  3  SELECT SUBSTR(MEMBER, 1, 70) "Name" FROM V$LOGFILE
  4  UNION
  5  SELECT SUBSTR(NAME, 1, 70) "Name"    FROM V$CONTROLFILE
  6* ORDER  BY  1
```

CONTROL FILES, DATABASE FILES, REDO LOG FILES, AND
INDEX FILES

```
Name
-------------------------------------------------------------
/home2/oracle/7.1.3/dbs/DES2_INDEXES_01.dbf
/home2/oracle/7.1.3/dbs/DES2_TABLES_01.dbf
/home2/oracle/7.1.3/dbs/ctrl1ora713.ctl
/home2/oracle/7.1.3/dbs/ctrl2ora713.ctl
/home2/oracle/7.1.3/dbs/ctrl3ora713.ctl
/home2/oracle/7.1.3/dbs/dbh_data1.dbf
/home2/oracle/7.1.3/dbs/dbh_index1.dbs
/home2/oracle/7.1.3/dbs/log1ora713.dbf
/home2/oracle/7.1.3/dbs/log2ora713.dbf
/home2/oracle/7.1.3/dbs/log3ora713.dbf
/home2/oracle/7.1.3/dbs/rbsora713.dbf
/home2/oracle/7.1.3/dbs/read_only.dbf
/home2/oracle/7.1.3/dbs/USER_data.dbf
/home2/oracle/7.1.3/dbs/USER_data2.dbf
/home2/oracle/7.1.3/dbs/USER_idx.dbf
/home2/oracle/7.1.3/dbs/systora713.dbf
/home2/oracle/7.1.3/dbs/systora713_2.dbf
/home2/oracle/7.1.3/dbs/systora713_3.dbf
/home2/oracle/7.1.3/dbs/temp2ora713.dbf
/home2/oracle/7.1.3/dbs/tempora713.dbf
/home2/oracle/7.1.3/dbs/tool2ora713.dbf
/home2/oracle/7.1.3/dbs/toolora713.dbf
/home2/oracle/7.1.3/dbs/usersora713.dbf
/home3/ora713/dbs/des2_rbs.dbf

24 rows selected.
```

Determining Your Rollback Segments

```
SQL> SELECT SUBSTR(NAME, 1, 25) "Name",
  2         SUBSTR(VALUE, 1, 30) "Value"
  3  FROM   V$PARAMETER  -- Look At Init.ora For Names
  4* WHERE  NAME LIKE '%' || lower('&Param') || '%';

Enter value for param: rollback_segments

Name                         Value
------------------------     ------------------------------
gc_rollback_segments         20
max_rollback_segments        30
rollback_segments            r01, r02, r03, r04
```

RBS=RRR=Rollback, Recovery, Read Consistency

```
SQL> get cb353
  1  COL     SEGMENT_NAME      FORMAT   A12
  2  COL     TABLESPACE_NAME   FORMAT   A15
  3  COL     STATUS            FORMAT   A7
  4  SELECT  SEGMENT_NAME,
  5          TABLESPACE_NAME,
  6          INITIAL_EXTENT INIT_X,
  7          NEXT_EXTENT NXT_X,
  8          MAX_EXTENTS MAX_X,
  9          STATUS
 10* FROM    SYS.DBA_ROLLBACK_SEGS
SQL> @cb353
```

SEGMENT_NAME	TABLESPACE_NAME	INIT_X	NXT_X	MAX_X	STATUS
SYSTEM	SYSTEM	51200	51200	121	ONLINE
DES2_RS1	DES2_RBS	1048576	1048576	121	OFFLINE
R01	RBS	131072	131072	121	ONLINE
R02	RBS	131072	131072	121	ONLINE
R03	RBS	131072	131072	121	ONLINE
R04	RBS	131072	131072	121	ONLINE
DES2_RS2	DES2_RBS	1048576	1048576	121	OFFLINE
DES2_RS3	DES2_RBS	1048576	1048576	121	OFFLINE

```
8 rows selected.
```

Building SQL*Plus DemoTables EMP, DEPT Etc.

Method 1:

```
>sqlplus student15/student15 @$ORACLE_HOME/sqlplus/demo/demobld
```

SQL*Plus: Release 3.1.3.4.1 - Production on Sun Aug 20 14:57:27 1995

Copyright (c) Oracle Corporation 1979, 1994. All rights reserved.

Connected to:
Oracle7 Server Release 7.1.3.0.0 - Production Release
With the distributed and parallel query options
PL/SQL Release 2.1.3.0.0 - Production

Building demonstration tables. Please wait.
Disconnected from Oracle7 Server Release 7.1.3.0.0 - Production Release
With the distributed and parallel query options
PL/SQL Release 2.1.3.0.0 - Production

Method 2:

SQL> @ $ORACLE_HOME/sqlplus/demo/demobld

Building demonstration tables. Please wait.

>

Notice with method 2, Oracle kicks you out of SQL*Plus back to your system prompt because of an *"exit"* command in demobld.sql.

On NT platforms this file might be in C:\ORANT\DBS.

Determining The Number Of Each Object Type

```
SQL> SELECT OBJECT_TYPE,
  2         COUNT(*)
  3  FROM   ALL_OBJECTS
  4  GROUP  BY OBJECT_TYPE;
```

```
OBJECT_TYPE     COUNT(*)
-----------   ----------
CLUSTER               1
INDEX                42
PACKAGE              14
PROCEDURE             3
SEQUENCE             26
SYNONYM            6218
TABLE               605
TRIGGER               1
VIEW                774

9 rows selected.
```

Determining The Current Settings Of Init.ora Parameters

```
SQL> SELECT  SUBSTR(NAME, 1, 35) "Name",
  2          SUBSTR(VALUE, 1, 15) "Value"
  3  FROM    V$PARAMETER
  4* WHERE   NAME LIKE '%' || lower('&Param') || '%'
SQL> /
Enter value for param: SHAR


Name                                  Value
-----------------------------------   ---------------
shared_pool_size                      18000000
```

You can also look at the file directly using your OS
commands. In passing, I have found the optimal size
for the shared_pool_size parameter is at least 7 meg. The
default of 3.5 meg is not nearly large enough.

> **more init.ora**

Or, if you can use SQLDBA,

SQLDBA> show parameter shar

Determining Which Init.ora Parameters Have Been Changed

```
SQL> SELECT COUNT(*)
  2  FROM    V$PARAMETER   -- How Many Have Been Changed
  3  WHERE   ISDEFAULT = 'FALSE';


COUNT(*)
--------
      45


SQL> SELECT SUBSTR(NAME, 1, 25) "Name",
  2          SUBSTR(VALUE,1, 30) "Value"
  3  FROM    V$PARAMETER -- Not Enough Room To See All 45
  4  WHERE   ISDEFAULT = 'FALSE' AND ROWNUM < 21
  5* ORDER   BY "Name";



Name                      Value
------------------------- ------------------------------
compatible                7.1.3
control_files             /home2/oracle/7.1.3/dbs/ctrl1o
db_block_buffers          200
db_block_size             2048
db_file_multiblock_read_c 8
db_files                  20
dml_locks                 100
enqueue_resources         120
gc_db_locks               200
log_archive_dest          ?/rdbms/log/arch
log_buffer                8192
log_checkpoint_interval   10000
log_simultaneous_copies   0
processes                 30
sessions                  38
shared_pool_size          18000000
temporary_table_locks     38
timed_statistics          TRUE
transactions              41
transactions_per_rollback 16

20 rows selected.
```

Determining Which DBMS Packages You Have

The BIG "O" wrote these packages for you to use. Most DBMS packages contain "work arounds". For example, the package DBMS_OUTPUT contains a procedure named PUT_LINE. PUT_LINE is used to display information to the terminal from within PL/SQL code.

```
SQL> SELECT OBJECT_NAME
  2  FROM    ALL_OBJECTS
  3  WHERE   OBJECT_NAME LIKE 'DBMS_%' AND
  4*         OBJECT_TYPE = 'PACKAGE';
```

```
OBJECT_NAME
------------------------------
DBMS_DDL
DBMS_DESCRIBE
DBMS_EXPORT_EXTENSION
DBMS_JOB
DBMS_OUTPUT
DBMS_REFRESH
DBMS_SESSION
DBMS_SNAPSHOT
DBMS_SQL
DBMS_STANDARD
DBMS_TRANSACTION
DBMS_UTILITY

12 rows selected.
```

Determining The Procedures In DBMS Packages

```
SQL> SELECT SUBSTR(TEXT, 1, 65) "Text"
  2  FROM    DBA_SOURCE
  3  WHERE   NAME = UPPER('&DBMS_Package') AND
  4          TEXT   LIKE  '%procedure%'    AND
  5          TEXT   NOT LIKE '%--%'
  6* ORDER   BY LINE;

Enter value for dbms_package: dbms_OUTPUT

Text
-----------------------------------------------------------------
  procedure enable (buffer_size in integer default 20000) is
  procedure disable is
  procedure put(a varchar2) is
  procedure put(a number) is
  procedure enable (buffer_size in integer default 20000);
  procedure put(a date) is
  procedure put_line(a varchar2) is
  procedure put_line(a number) is
  procedure disable;
  procedure put(a varchar2);
  procedure put(a number);
  procedure put(a date);
  procedure put_line(a date) is
  procedure new_line is
  procedure put_line(a varchar2);
  procedure put_line(a number);
  procedure put_line(a date);
  procedure new_line;
  procedure get_line(line out varchar2, status out integer);
  procedure get_line(line out varchar2, status out integer)
is
  procedure get_lines(lines out chararr, numlines in out
integer)
  procedure get_lines(lines out chararr, numlines in out
integer)
22 rows selected.
```

Entering SQL> **DESC DBMS_OUTPUT** also displays the functions and procedures in a package.

Determining The Location Of SQL Trace Dump Files

```
SQL> GET cb358
  1   SELECT  SUBSTR(NAME,   1,   20) "Name",
  2           SUBSTR(VALUE,  1,   37) "Value"
  3   FROM    V$PARAMETER
  4*  WHERE   NAME LIKE '%' || lower('&Param') || '%'
SQL> /

Enter value for param: user_dump_dest


Name                 Value
-------------------- -------------------------------------
user_dump_dest       /home2/oracle/7.1.3/rdbms/log
```

Determining How Many Extents Are In A Table

Remember, **"Fewer And Larger"** extents is your goal with Oracle tables. Looks like you have a real performance problem on the BIG table because of so many extents.

```
SQL> GET cb351
  1   SELECT MAX(EXTENT_ID) "Number Of Extents"
  2   FROM    SYS.DBA_EXTENTS
  3   WHERE   OWNER         =    UPPER('&Owner')    AND
  4           SEGMENT_TYPE =    UPPER('&SegType') AND
  5*          SEGMENT_NAME = upper('&SegName')
SQL> /
Enter value for owner: student15
Enter value for segtype: table
Enter value for segname: big

Number Of Extents
-----------------
               61
```

The following query identifies objects within 2 extents of the maximum extent setting for the object. As we say in Texas, "Objects you are fixin to hit the maximum extent size".

```
SQL> SELECT SUBSTR(SEGMENT_NAME,1,15) "Segment Name",
  2          EXTENTS
  3   FROM    DBA_SEGMENTS
  3*  WHERE   EXTENTS + 3 > MAX_EXTENTS;

Segment Name        EXTENTS
---------------     ---------
IRL                        2
```

Changing Your Password

Method 1: (Changed by the user)

```
SQL> ALTER USER STUDENT15
  2          IDENTIFIED BY INDY500;
```

User altered.

```
SQL> CONNECT STUDENT15/INDY500
```

Connected.

Method 2: (Changed by the DBA)

```
SQL> ALTER USER STUDENT15
          IDENTIFIED BY INDY500;
```

User altered.

OR

```
SQL> GRANT CONNECT TO STUDENT15 IDENTIFIED BY INDY500;
```

Connected.

Exceeding Your Profile Limit

```
SQL> CONNECT SYSTEM/MANAGER
Connected.
SQL> CREATE PROFILE FIVE_MIN LIMIT
  2          CONNECT_TIME      5
  3          IDLE_TIME         5;
Profile created.
SQL> ALTER SYSTEM SET RESOURCE_LIMIT = TRUE;
System altered.

SQL> SET TIME ON
16:47:02 SQL> ALTER USER STUDENT3 PROFILE FIVE_MIN;
User altered.

16:50:20 SQL> CONNECT STUDENT3/STUDENT3
Connected.

16:50:57 SQL> -- TAKE A BREAK, YOU LOOK LIKE YOU NEED ONE

16:51:09 SQL> SELECT *
17:01:20   2  FROM    DEPT;
SELECT *
*
ERROR at line 1:
ORA-02396: exceeded maximum idle time, please connect again


17:01:30 SQL> CONNECT STUDENT3/STUDENT3
Connected.

         SQL> -- ENTER COMMANDS FOR FIVE MINUTES

17:06:46 SQL> L
  1* SELECT * FROM EMP
07:53:48 SQL> /
ERROR:
ORA-02399:exceeded maximum connect time,you are being logged
off
```

Getting Help On Non NT Platforms

`SQL> HELP MENU` -- DISPLAYS THE MAIN MENU OF HELP TOPICS

`SQL> HELP COMMANDS` -- LIST OF SQL*Plus, SQL, AND PL/SQL
    i.e. `SQL> HELP ALTER TABLE`

`SQL> HELP COMM` -- INFO ON COMMANDS, COMMENTS, AND COMMIT

`SQL> HELP HELP` -- DISPLAYS SCREEN ON ONE WAY TO USE HELP

`SQL> HELP LIMITS` -- TO SEE THE LIMITS OF YOUR SYSTEM

```
Limits
  Item                               SQL*Plus Limit
  -----------------------------------------------------
  file name length                   system-dependent
  username length                    30  characters
  user variable name length          30  characters
  user variable value length         240 characters
  number of user variables           1,024
  variables in INSERT INTO list      50
  variables per SQL command          100
  command line length                500 characters
  length of LONG value in SQL*Plus   2 gigabytes
  LONGCHUNKSIZE value (Oracle7)      MAXDATA value
  MAXDATA value                      system-dependent
  output line size   500 characters (minimum  = 5 characters)
  line after variable substitution 1,000 characters (internal
only)
  number of lines per command        500 (assuming 80
characters per line)
  number of lines per page           50,000
  total row width                    60,000 characters in
VMS; else, 32,767
  rows in an array fetch             5000 rows
  nested command files               20 for VMS, CMS, Unix;
otherwise, 5
  page numbers                       99,999 pages
  ACCEPT CHAR                        98 bytes

  See also:  commands, menu.
```

Determining Table Constraints

```
SQL> SET      VERIFY              OFF
SQL> COL      CONSTRAINT_NAME     FORMAT A16
SQL> COL      CONSTRAINT_TYPE     FORMAT A15
SQL> COL      SEARCH_CONDITION    FORMAT A20


SQL> SELECT CONSTRAINT_NAME,
  2          CONSTRAINT_TYPE,
  3          SEARCH_CONDITION
  4   FROM   USER_CONSTRAINTS
  5   WHERE  TABLE_NAME = UPPER('&Table');
Enter value for table: dept

CONSTRAINT_NAME   CONSTRAINT_TYPE SEARCH_CONDITION
----------------  --------------- --------------------
PK_DEPT_DEPTNO    P
UN_DEPT_DNAME     U
CK_DEPT_LOC       C                 LOC NOT IN('MAUI')

Constraint Types:

P = Primary Key
R = Foreign Key (Referential Integrity)
U = Unique
C = Check Or Not Null
```

There are other constraint types besides the four listed above: A constraint type of "V" for views created with the CHECK OPTION, and a constraint type of "O" for LOBs in Oracle8 and Oracle8i.

```
SQL> COL CONSTRAINT_TYPE FORMAT A15
SQL> SELECT DISTINCT(CONSTRAINT_TYPE)
  2* FROM   DBA_CONSTRAINTS;

CONSTRAINT_TYPE
---------------
C
O
P
R
U
V
```

Determining How Many Rows In A Table

```
Method 1:

SQL> SELECT COUNT(*)
  2  FROM    EMP;
COUNT(*)
--------
      14


Method 2:

SQL> SELECT NUM_ROWS      -- Table Not Analyzed If NUM_ROWS
  2  FROM    USER_TABLES  -- Is Null
  3  WHERE   TABLE_NAME = UPPER('&Table');
Enter value for table: emp
NUM_ROWS
--------


SQL> ANALYZE TABLE EMP COMPUTE STATISTICS;
Table analyzed.

SQL> SELECT NUM_ROWS
  2  FROM    USER_TABLES
  3* WHERE   TABLE_NAME = UPPER('&Table');

Enter value for table: emp
NUM_ROWS
--------
      14


Method 3: (Very Fast For Large Tables - Use PK Index)

SQL> SELECT --+ RULE
  2              COUNT(*)
  3  FROM        EMP
  4* WHERE       EMPNO > 0;

 COUNT(*)
--------
      14
```

Determining How Many Columns In A Table

```
SQL> SELECT COUNT(*) "Number Of Columns"
  2  FROM   ALL_TAB_COLUMNS
  3  WHERE  OWNER = UPPER('&Owner') AND
  4*         TABLE_NAME = UPPER('&Table');
```

Enter value for table: **EMP**

```
Number Of Columns
-----------------
                8
```

SQL> DESC EMP

Name	Null?	Type
EMPNO	NOT NULL	NUMBER(4)
ENAME		VARCHAR2(10)
JOB		VARCHAR2(9)
MGR		NUMBER(4)
HIREDATE		DATE
SAL		NUMBER(7,2)
COMM		NUMBER(7,2)
DEPTNO		NUMBER(2)

Notice EMP does have eight columns.

SQL> SHOW USER
user is "STUDENT15"

Column Defaults

```
SQL> ALTER TABLE    EMP
          MODIFY   SAL
          DEFAULT 1900;
Table altered.
.
.
.   etc. etc.


SQL> COL COLUMN_NAME    FORMAT A12
SQL> COL DATA_DEFAULT   FORMAT A20


SQL> SELECT COLUMN_NAME,
  2         DATA_DEFAULT
  3  FROM    USER_TAB_COLUMNS
  4  WHERE   TABLE_NAME = UPPER('&Table');

Enter value for table: emp


COLUMN_NAME   DATA_DEFAULT
-----------   --------------------
EMPNO
ENAME
JOB           'CLERK'
MGR
HIREDATE
SAL           1900
COMM
DEPTNO        10

8 rows selected.
```

Determining Actual Data Length Of Character Columns

```
SQL> SELECT MAX(LENGTH(USERNAME)) "Max Username",
  2  MAX(LENGTH(DEFAULT_TABLESPACE)) "Max Tablespace",
  3  MAX(LENGTH(TEMPORARY_TABLESPACE)) "Max Temp Tablespace"
  4  FROM   USER_USERS;

Max Username Max Tablespace Max Temp Tablespace
------------ -------------- -------------------
           8             15                   7
```

```
SQL> SELECT USERNAME, DEFAULT_TABLESPACE,
  2           TEMPORARY_TABLESPACE
  3  FROM   USER_USERS;

USERNAME DEFAULT_TABLESPACE TEMPORARY_TABLESPACE
-------- ------------------ --------------------
STUDENT3 TRAINING_TABLES    TEMP_TS
```

```
Notice that the length of USERNAME student3 is 8.
The length of DEFAULT_TABLESPACE training_tables is 15.
The length of TEMPORARY_TABLESPACE temp_ts is 7.
```

```
Therefore, you know exactly how to format the
columns in this table - without guessing.
```

```
SQL> COL USERNAME             FORMAT A8
SQL> COL DEFAULT_TABLESPACE    FORMAT A15 HEADING 'DEF TS'
SQL> COL TEMPORARY_TABLESPACE  FORMAT A7 HEADING 'TEMP TS'
```

Detecting "Chaining" In A Table

```
SQL> @ $ORACLE_HOME/rdbms/admin/utlchain
SQL> -- This script builds the table named "CHAINED_ROWS"
SQL> create table CHAINED_ROWS (
  2     owner_name          varchar2(30),
  3     table_name          varchar2(30),
  4     cluster_name        varchar2(30),
  5     head_rowid          rowid,
  6     timestamp           date
  7  );
Table created.

SQL> ANALYZE TABLE EMP LIST CHAINED ROWS;
Table analyzed.

SQL> SELECT COUNT(*) -- WOW DUDE..LIKE LOTS OF CHAINING
  2  FROM    CHAINED_ROWS;
COUNT(*)
--------
     104

SQL> SELECT OWNER_NAME, TABLE_NAME, HEAD_ROWID
  2  FROM    CHAINED_ROWS
  3* WHERE   ROWNUM < 2;

OWNER_NAME TABLE_NAME HEAD_ROWID          TIMESTAMP
---------- ---------- ------------------- ---------
STUDENT3   EMP        000005CB.0001.0003  22-AUG-95

SQL> SELECT EMPNO, ENAME  -- 7499 To Limit # Rows Returned
  2  FROM    EMP,   CHAINED_ROWS CR
  3  WHERE   EMP.ROWID = CR.HEAD_ROWID AND EMPNO = 7499;
  EMPNO ENAME
------- ----------
   7499 ALLEN
```

> As one singer says,"Whole Lottah Chainin Goin On!"
> Contact your nearest DBA. This could be one reason your
> ad hoc queries against this table have to shift up three
> speeds just to be stopped.

If You Receive A Message From Diana

```
SQL> SELECT
  2   ENAME
  3   (SAL + COMM)
  4   FROM EMP;
FROM EMP
     *
ERROR at line 4:
ORA-04028: cannot generate diana for object STUDENT3.EMP
```

```
SQL> !oerr ora 4028
04028, 00000, "cannot generate diana for object %s%s%s%s%s"
// *Cause:  Cannot generate diana for an object because of
lock conflict.
// *Action: Please report this error to your support
representative.
```

```
Diana is a package written by Oracle.
```

Commenting Your SQL Statements

```
SQL> get comments
  1   REM   The REM Is Short For REMARK
  2   SELECT MAX(SAL)    /*  Highest Mon Sal Dept 20  */
  3   FROM    EMP        --  I Prefer This Way Of Commenting
  4   WHERE   DEPTNO  =  20
SQL> @comments

MAX(SAL)
--------
    3000

1 row selected.
```

Because I have a tinge of dyslexia, you can certainly understand why my favorite comment is "--". No way I can get that one mixed up.

Have you heard of the group called M.A.D.D. (Mothers Against Drunk Drivers) ? I heard the other day a new group has been formed called D.A.M. (**M**others **A**gainst **D**yslexia)

CHAPTER

2

Morning Snack
Or
Pseudo Columns

Determining Your User ID (UID)

Method 1:

```
SQL> SELECT UID
  2  FROM    DUAL;

    UID
-------
     40
```

Method 2:

```
SQL> SELECT USER_ID
  2  FROM    USER_USERS;

USER_ID
-------
     40
```

Using Nextval And Currval

```
SQL> CREATE SEQUENCE FOR_DEPT   -- DON'T WANT GAPS
  2         START    WITH    41 -- USE NOCACHE
  3         NOCACHE;
Sequence created.

SQL> SELECT * FROM DEPT;
 DEPTNO DNAME          LOC
------- -------------- -------------
     10 ACCOUNTING     NEW YORK
     20 RESEARCH       DALLAS
     30 SALES          CHICAGO
     40 OPERATIONS     BOSTON

SQL> INSERT INTO DEPT
  2*        VALUES(FOR_DEPT.NEXTVAL, 'IS', 'HANA');

1 row created.
SQL> SELECT * FROM DEPT;
 DEPTNO DNAME          LOC
------- -------------- -------------
     10 ACCOUNTING     NEW YORK
     20 RESEARCH       DALLAS
     30 SALES          CHICAGO
     40 OPERATIONS     BOSTON
     41 IS             HANA

1  SELECT   FOR_DEPT.CURRVAL
2* FROM     DUAL
SQL> /

CURRVAL
-------
     41

SQL*Forms PRE-INSERT Trigger

SELECT FOR_DEPT.NEXTVAL
INTO   :DEPT.DEPTNO
FROM   DUAL;
```

Using Sysdate

```
SQL> SELECT SYSDATE
  2  FROM    DUAL;
SYSDATE
---------
23-AUG-95
SQL> SELECT TO_CHAR(SYSDATE, 'HH:MI:SS') "Hr Min Sec"
  2  FROM    DUAL;
 Hr Min Sec
------------------------------------------------------------
10:15:29
SQL> INSERT INTO EMP(EMPNO,ENAME,HIREDATE) -- Actual Time
  2          VALUES(5555, 'THE PISTOL', SYSDATE);
1 row created.

SQL> INSERT INTO EMP(EMPNO,ENAME,HIREDATE) -- 12:00:00
  2          VALUES(7777, 'THE DUKE', '23-AUG-95');
1 row created.

SQL> SELECT ENAME, HIREDATE
  2  FROM    EMP
  3  WHERE   HIREDATE = '23-AUG-95';
ENAME      HIREDATE
---------- ---------
THE DUKE   23-AUG-95
SQL> -- WHAT HAPPENED TO "THE PISTOL" PETE ???

SQL> SELECT ENAME,HIREDATE,
            TO_CHAR(HIREDATE,'HH:MI:SS') "Time"
  2  FROM    EMP
  3  WHERE   HIREDATE LIKE '23-AUG-95';
ENAME      HIREDATE  Time
---------- --------- --------
THE PISTOL 23-AUG-95 10:48:59
THE DUKE   23-AUG-95 12:00:00

SQL> SELECT ENAME,HIREDATE,
            TO_CHAR(HIREDATE, 'HH:MI:SS') "Time"
  2  FROM    EMP
  3  WHERE TRUNC(HIREDATE) = '23-AUG-95';

ENAME      HIREDATE  Time
---------- --------- --------
THE PISTOL 23-AUG-95 10:48:59
THE DUKE   23-AUG-95 12:00:00
```

> So, use **TRUNC** or **LIKE** to retrieve them all if you are using SYSDATE for date data.

Another Use Of Sysdate

```
SQL> SELECT SYSDATE + 121   -- What Will The Date Be 121 Days
  2  FROM    DUAL;          -- From Now ?

SYSDATE+1
---------
25-DEC-95

SQL>  SELECT ENAME,
  2    HIREDATE,
  3    TRUNC(SYSDATE - HIREDATE) "Days",
  4    TRUNC((SYSDATE - HIREDATE)/7) "Weeks",
  5    TRUNC(MONTHS_BETWEEN(SYSDATE, HIREDATE)) "Mos",
  6    TRUNC((MONTHS_BETWEEN(SYSDATE, HIREDATE))/12) "Years"
  7  FROM    EMP            -- Only Want To See One Row
  8* WHERE   ROWNUM < 2;


ENAME       HIREDATE  Days Weeks Mos Years
-----       --------- ---- ----- --- -----
SMITH       17-DEC-80 5365   766 176    14
```

To determine how old a person is who was born on 11-DEC-50, you can do the following, or you can even prompt for the birthday with '&DOB'.

```
SQL> COL "Days Old" FORMAT 99,999
SQL> SELECT
  2  TRUNC(SYSDATE-TO_DATE('12/11/50','MM/DD/YY')) "Days Old"
  3  FROM   DUAL;

 Days Old
----------
   16,329
```

Using Rowid(Oracle7)

To Retrieve A Row The Quickest Way Possible

i.e.   Say you are constantly retrieving the President
of your company, and even with an index on the job
column, performance is not good. Assuming your DBA
does not perform frequent EXPORTs and IMPORTS, which
changes the ROWIDs, you can determine the ROWID for
the PRESIDENT, and use it.

```
SQL> SELECT ROWID, ENAME, JOB
  2  FROM    EMP
  3  WHERE   JOB = 'PRESIDENT';
```

```
ROWID                 ENAME      JOB
------------------    ----------  ---------
000005DF.0008.0003  KING        PRESIDENT
```

```
SQL> SELECT ENAME, JOB, SAL
  2  FROM    EMP
  3  WHERE   ROWID = '000005DF.0008.0003';
```

```
ENAME      JOB          SAL
----------  ---------   ----------
KING        PRESIDENT    5000
```

To determine the approximate number of blocks in a table:

```
SQL> SELECT COUNT(DISTINCT   -- Approximate # Of Blocks
               SUBSTR(ROWID, 1, 8) ||
               SUBSTR(ROWID, 15, 4)) BLKS
  2* FROM    BIGGER;
```

```
    BLKS
----------
      66
```

You can also ANALYZE a table and sum the BLOCKS and
EMPTY_BLOCKS columns of USER_TABLES, to calculate the number
of blocks in a table. Analyzing the table works much better
in Oracle8 and Oracle8i.

Using Rownum

```
SQL> SELECT *         -- Just Want To See A Couple Of Rows
  2  FROM    EMP
  3* WHERE   ROWNUM < 3
SQL> /


EMPNO ENAME JOB          MGR HIREDATE    SAL COMM  DEPTNO
----- ----- --------    ---- --------   ---- ----  -------
7369  SMITH CLERK       7902 17-DEC-80  800            20
7499  ALLEN SALESMAN    7698 20-FEB-81 1600  300        30




SQL> CREATE TABLE EMP_TEST AS  -- CREATE TABLE WITH 4 ROWS
  2         SELECT *
  3         FROM    EMP
  4         WHERE   ROWNUM < 5;

Table created.


SQL> SELECT *
  2  FROM    EMP_TEST;


EMPNO ENAME JOB          MGR HIREDATE   SAL  COMM DEPTNO
----- ----- --------    ---- --------  ---- ---- ------
 7369 SMITH CLERK       7902 17-DEC-80  800           20
 7499 ALLEN SALESMAN    7698 20-FEB-81 1600  300       30
 7521 WARD  SALESMAN    7698 22-FEB-81 1250  500       30
 7566 JONES MANAGER     7839 02-APR-81 2975           20
```

Using Level

```
SQL> COL Hierarchy FORMAT A18
SQL> SELECT  LPAD(' ',3*LEVEL) || ENAME Hierarchy
  2  FROM     EMP        -- LEVEL WITH LPAD CAUSES INDENTATION
  3  CONNECT BY PRIOR EMPNO = MGR
  4* START   WITH JOB       = 'PRESIDENT';

HIERARCHY
------------------
   KING
      JONES
         SCOTT
            ADAMS
         FORD
            SMITH
      BLAKE
         ALLEN
         WARD
         MARTIN
         TURNER
         JAMES
      CLARK
         MILLER
14 rows selected.

SQL> get cb55
  1  COL    "Query Plan"              FORMAT A52
  2  SELECT LPAD(' ',2*(LEVEL-1))        ||
  3         OPERATION            || ' ' ||
  4         OPTIONS              || ' ' ||
  5         OBJECT_NAME          || ' ' ||
  6         DECODE(ID,0,'Cost = ' || POSITION) ||
  7         ' Optimizer = '      || OPTIMIZER "Query Plan"
  8  FROM   PLAN_TABLE
  9  START  WITH ID     = 0
 10* CONNECT BY PRIOR ID = PARENT_ID
SQL> @cb55

Query Plan
-------------------------------------------------------
SELECT STATEMENT    Cost = 382 Optimizer = CHOOSE
  TABLE ACCESS FULL BIG  Optimizer = ANALYZED
```

CHAPTER

3

Coffee Break (Le Pause Cafe´)
Or
Environmental
Parameters

Using Accept

Method 1:(Hey Ma, look! No prompts in the SQL stmt)

SQL> ACCEPT DNO PROMPT 'Please Enter Department Number: '
Please Enter Department Number: **20**

```
SQL> SELECT *
  2   FROM    EMP
  3   WHERE   DEPTNO = &DNO;
```

EMPNO	ENAME	JOB	MGR	HIREDATE	SAL	COMM	DEPTNO
7369	SMITH	CLERK	7902	17-DEC-80	800		**20**
7566	JONES	MANAGER	7839	02-APR-81	2975		**20**
7788	SCOTT	ANALYST	7566	09-DEC-82	3000		**20**
7876	ADAMS	CLERK	7788	12-JAN-83	1100		**20**
7902	FORD	ANALYST	7566	03-DEC-81	3000		**20**

Method 2:   Prompt With A Percent Sign

SQL> ACCEPT X PROMPT 'Enter Dept %%'
Enter Dept **%10**
SQL> def x
*DEFINE X   = **"10"** (CHAR)*

Method 3:

SQL> DEFINE TEXT='Please Enter Dept %'
SQL> ACCEPT X PROMPT '&TEXT %'
Please Enter Dept **%20**
SQL> DEF X
*DEFINE X   = **"20"** (CHAR)*
SQL> DEF TEXT
DEFINE TEXT   = "Please Enter Dept %" (CHAR)

Using Double &&

```
SQL>  UNDEFINE CITY            -- Must Do This After First Run
SQL>  L                        -- Or You Will Not Get Prompted
  1   SELECT  ENAME &&City      -- Ever Again !!!
  2   FROM    EMP,    DEPT
  3   WHERE   EMP.DEPTNO = DEPT.DEPTNO AND
  4*          LOC        = '&City'
SQL>  /
Enter value for city: DALLAS
old   1: SELECT  ENAME &&City
new   1: SELECT  ENAME DALLAS
old   4:          LOC       = '&City'
new   4:          LOC       = 'DALLAS'


DALLAS
----------
SMITH
ADAMS
FORD
SCOTT
JONES




SQL>  SELECT  ENAME, LOC       -- To Verify Our Results
  2   FROM    EMP,    DEPT
  3   WHERE   EMP.DEPTNO = DEPT.DEPTNO AND
  4           LOC        = 'DALLAS';

ENAME       LOC
----------  --------------
SMITH       DALLAS
ADAMS       DALLAS
FORD        DALLAS
SCOTT       DALLAS
JONES       DALLAS
```

Another Way To Use &&

```
SQL> SELECT *
  2  FROM    EMP
  3* WHERE   ENAME = 'BLAKE';
```

```
EMPNO ENAME JOB       MGR HIREDATE    SAL COMM DEPTNO
----- ----- ------- ---- --------- ----- ---- ------
 7698 BLAKE MANAGER 7839 01-MAY-81  2850          30
```

```
SQL> INSERT INTO EMP(EMPNO,ENAME,JOB,HIREDATE,SAL)
  2  VALUES(4444,'BIG BUCKS','MANAGER','30-JUN-91',4275);
```

1 row created.

Blake thinks his merit increase and salary is a tad bit too small. Let's write a query to see if management overlooked him. He is right !

```
SQL> UNDEFINE NAME
SQL> SELECT *
  2  FROM    EMP
  3  WHERE   SAL     >   (SELECT SAL
  4                         FROM    EMP
  5                         WHERE   ENAME = '&&Name') AND
  6         JOB      =   (SELECT JOB
  7                         FROM    EMP
  8                         WHERE   ENAME = '&Name')   AND
  9      HIREDATE    >   (SELECT HIREDATE
 10                         FROM    EMP
 11                         WHERE   ENAME = '&Name');
```
Enter value for name: **BLAKE**

```
EMPNO ENAME        JOB      MGR HIREDATE    SAL COMM DEPTNO
----- --------- ------- --- -------- ---- ---- ------
 4444 BIG BUCKS MANAGER     30-JUN-91 4275
I wonder if BIG BUCKS has lots of doe ?
```

Using Array Processing

SQL*Plus

```
SQL> SHOW ARRAYSIZE
arraysize 15
```

SQL*Loader

```
>sqlload wham/bam thank_you.ctl rows=200
```

PRO* Products (Pre-compilers)

```
EXEC SQL INSERT INTO SALES(SALES_ID)
        VALUES(:SID);
```

```
Where :SID is an integer array, variable length data, and
one hundred elements.
```

OCI's (Oracle Call Interfaces)

```
OEXN Call
OFEN Call
```

Export/Import

```
>exp userid=student15/student15 tables=emp buffer=40960
```

SQL*Forms V3.0

```
Array Size: [ ]
```

Using Array Processing In SQL*Plus

```
SQL> CREATE   TABLE   TOO_WIDE
  2      (COL1 VARCHAR2(2000),
  3       COL2 VARCHAR2(1500),
  4       COL3 VARCHAR2(1800),
  5       COL4 VARCHAR2(2000));
```

Table created.

```
SQL> SELECT * FROM TOO_WIDE;
```
buffer overflow. Use SET command to reduce **ARRAYSIZE** *or increase MAXDATA.*

```
SQL> SHOW ARRAYSIZE
```
arraysize 15

```
SQL> SET ARRAYSIZE 9
SQL> /
```
buffer overflow. Use SET command to reduce **ARRAYSIZE** *or increase MAXDATA.*

```
SQL> SET ARRAYSIZE 8
SQL> /
```

no rows selected

For tables with many columns or tables with wide columns like above in table TOO_WIDE, you must DECREASE the arraysize to perform queries etc. on the table.

Oracle's financial applications are filled with tables comprised of anywhere from 2 to 90 columns per table.

Bind Variables &DNO, :DNO, And :ORD.DNO

SQL*Plus

```
SQL> TTITLE 'Keystone Steel & Widgets'
Enter value for widgets: Weird Dude
SQL> SET SCAN OFF
SQL> SELECT *
  2  FROM    EMP
  3  WHERE   DEPTNO = &DNO;
Bind variable "DNO" not declared.
```

PRO*Products (Pre-compilers)

```
EXEC SQL
    SELECT ENAME
    INTO   :NAME
    FROM   EMP
    WHERE  EMPNO = 7902;
```

SQL*Forms

```
SELECT NAME
INTO   :ORD.CNAME
FROM   CUSTOMER
WHERE  :ORD.CUSTID = CUSTID;
```

Using Define

Thanks to my students in Richmond, Virginia for asking if you can do this in Oracle to save yourself a lot of typing.

```
SQL> DEF X=NVL(SAL,0)+NVL(COMM,0)


SQL> L
  1  SELECT  ENAME, SAL, COMM, &X TS, &X + 300 SAL_PLUS
  2* FROM    EMP
SQL> /
```

ENAME	SAL	COMM	TS	SAL_PLUS
SMITH	800		800	1100
ALLEN	1600	300	1900	2200
WARD	1250	500	1750	2050
JONES	2975		2975	3275
MARTIN	1250	1400	2650	2950
BLAKE	2850		2850	3150
CLARK	2450		2450	2750
SCOTT	3000		3000	3300
KING	5000		5000	5300
TURNER	1500	0	1500	1800
ADAMS	1100		1100	1400
JAMES	950		950	1250
FORD	3000		3000	3300
MILLER	1300		1300	1600
THE PISTOL			0	300
THE DUKE			0	300
BIG BUCKS	4275		4275	4575

17 rows selected.

Using Define In The "SHOW" & "SET DEFINE" Commands

Thanks to some folks in Peoria, we discovered this little gem. Seems as though they needed to see a "&" in the top title of their reports. But every time they tried the ttitle command with an ampersand, it prompted them.

Method 1:

```
SQL> SHOW DEFINE
define "&" (hex 26)
SQL> SET DEFINE "?"
SQL> TTITLE 'Keystone Steal & Bases'
SQL> SELECT ENAME, SAL
  2  FROM   EMP;
```

```
Wed Aug 23                                              page    1
                     Keystone Steal & Bases


ENAME          SAL
---------- -------
SMITH          800
```

Method 2:

```
SQL> SET DEFINE "?"
SQL> SET HEADING OFF
SQL> SELECT 'Keystone Cops & Robbers'
  2  FROM    DUAL;
 Keystone Cops & Robbers

SQL> SET HEADING ON
SQL> SET DEFINE "&"
SQL> DEFINE X=NVL(SAL,0)+500
SQL> SELECT ENAME, SAL, &X SAL_PLUS_500
  2  FROM    EMP;
old    1: SELECT ENAME, SAL, &X SAL_PLUS_500
new    1: SELECT ENAME, SAL, NVL(SAL,0)+500 SAL_PLUS_500


ENAME          SAL SAL_PLUS_500
-----          --- ------------
SMITH          800         1300
```

Using Define With Rowid

```
SQL> SELECT ROWID, ENAME
  2  FROM    EMP
  3* WHERE   JOB = 'PRESIDENT';


ROWID                  ENAME
------------------ ----------
000005DF.0008.0003 KING



SQL> DEFINE X='000005DF.0008.0003'

SQL> SET VERIFY OFF

SQL> SELECT ENAME, JOB, SAL
  2  FROM    EMP
  3  WHERE   ROWID = '&X';
old   3: WHERE   ROWID = '&X'
new   3: WHERE   ROWID = '000005DF.0008.0003'


ENAME      JOB              SAL
---------- --------- ----------
KING       PRESIDENT       5000
```

Specifying Editors

```
SQL> DEF
DEFINE _O_VERSION       = "Oracle7 Server Release 7.1.4.1.0 -
Production Release
With the distributed and parallel query options
PL/SQL Release 2.1.4.0.0 - Production" (CHAR)
DEFINE _O_RELEASE       = "701040100" (CHAR)


SQL> DEF _EDITOR=vi


SQL> DEF
DEFINE _O_VERSION       = "Oracle7 Server Release 7.1.4.1.0 -
Production Release
With the distributed and parallel query options
PL/SQL Release 2.1.4.0.0 - Production" (CHAR)
DEFINE _O_RELEASE       = "701040100" (CHAR)
DEFINE X                = "000005DF.0008.0003" (CHAR)
DEFINE _EDITOR          = "vi" (CHAR)
```

Depending on your platform type, you can also enter:

```
SQL> def _editor=notepad.exe    (PC's)

SQL> def _editor=emacs          (Unix Boxes)

SQL> def _editor=edt            (VMS)

SQL> def _editor=eve            (VMS)
```

So you don't have to enter this command every time
you log on to SQL*Plus, place the above line of code in your
login.sql file.

Using Feedback

```
SQL> SHOW FEEDBACK
feedback ON for 6 or more rows

SQL> SELECT ENAME, SAL
  2  FROM    EMP
  3  WHERE   SAL > 1800;

ENAME              SAL
---------- ----------
JONES             2975
BLAKE             2850
CLARK             2450
SCOTT             3000
KING              5000
FORD              3000
BIG BUCKS         4275


7 rows selected.

SQL> CREATE SYNONYM PISTOL FOR EMP;
Synonym created.

SQL> SET FEEDBACK OFF
SQL> SELECT ENAME, SAL  -- Notice No "7 rows selected"
  2  FROM    EMP
  3  WHERE   SAL > 1900;
ENAME              SAL
---------- ----------
JONES             2975
BLAKE             2850
CLARK             2450
SCOTT             3000
KING              5000
FORD              3000
BIG BUCKS         4275


SQL> DROP SYNONYM PISTOL;
Notice no message of "Synonym dropped.".
```

Using Long

```
SQL> CREATE VIEW POSITIVE AS
  2   SELECT  EMPNO,ENAME,JOB,SAL,COMM,MGR,DEPT.DEPTNO DNO,
  3           HIREDATE,DNAME,LOC
  4           FROM    EMP, DEPT
  5*          WHERE   EMP.DEPTNO = DEPT.DEPTNO;

View created.

SQL> SHOW LONG
long 80

SQL> COL VIEW_NAME          FORMAT      A10
SQL> SELECT VIEW_NAME,
  2          TEXT
  3   FROM    USER_VIEWS
  4   WHERE   VIEW_NAME = 'POSITIVE';


VIEW_NAME
----------
TEXT
----------------------------------------------------------------
POSITIVE
SELECT EMPNO, ENAME, JOB, SAL, COMM, MGR, DEPT.DEPTNO DNO,
            HIREDAT
SQL> SET LONG 160
SQL> SELECT VIEW_NAME,
  2          TEXT
  3   FROM    USER_VIEWS
  4   WHERE   VIEW_NAME = 'POSITIVE';


VIEW_NAME
----------
TEXT
----------------------------------------------------------------
POSITIVE
SELECT EMPNO, ENAME, JOB, SAL, COMM, MGR, DEPT.DEPTNO DNO,
            HIREDATE, DNAME, LOC
      FROM    EMP, DEPT
      WHERE   EMP.DEPTNO = DEPT.DEPTNO

Notice no truncation of "TEXT" this time since LONG = 160.
```

Using Null

```
SQL> SHOW NULL
null ""

SQL> SET NULL Nada

SQL> l
  1  SELECT  ENAME, SAL, COMM
  2  FROM    EMP
  3* WHERE   JOB <> 'SALESMAN' AND ROWNUM < 2
SQL> /


ENAME               SAL       COMM
---------- ---------- ----------
SMITH               800 Nada


SQL> UPDATE EMP     -- SET FORD's NAME TO A NULL
  2          SET ENAME = ''
  3          WHERE ENAME = 'FORD';

1 row updated.

SQL> COL ENAME NULL +


SQL> l
  1  SELECT ENAME, JOB, SAL, COMM   -- Nada In COMM And
  2  FROM    EMP                    -- "+" In Ename If Null
  3* WHERE ENAME IS NULL OR ENAME = 'SMITH'
SQL> /

ENAME      JOB             SAL       COMM
---------- ---------- ---------- ----------
SMITH      CLERK           800 Nada
+          ANALYST        3000 Nada
```

Using Spool

```
Method 1:  Are We Spooling ?
SQL> SPOOL
not spooling currently

Method 2:  Let's Spool All Of Our Environment Variables
           to a disk file, and look at the file.
SQL> SPOOL env.lis          -- Starts Spooling To env.lis
SQL> SHOW ALL               -- All Env Variables & Settings
SQL> SPOOL OFF              -- Stop Spooling & Close env.lis
SQL> host more env.lis      -- A Way To Look At env.lis
SQL> !more env.lis          -- Another Way To Look At env.lis

Method 3:  To print the report on your own printer instead
           of the system printer, spool to a file, run your
           report, turn the spooler off, and then print the
           file using the appropriate os command.
SQL> SPOOL daily_rep.lis
SQL> START daily.sql
SQL> SPOOL OFF
SQL> host lpr -Pdallas1 daily_rep.lis           -- Unix
SQL> !lpr -Pdallas1 daily_rep.lis               -- Unix
SQL> HOST PRINT/QUE=DALLAS1 DAILY_REP.LIS        -- VMS
SQL> $PRINT/QUE=DALLAS1 DAILY_REP.LIS            -- VMS

Method 4:  Send a report to the system default printer.
SQL> SPOOL daily_rep.lis
SQL> @daily.lis
ENAME          SAL
---------- -------
SMITH          800
SQL> SPOOL OUT              -- Closes daily_rep.lis & Sends
                           -- To The System Printer
Method 5:  Write all of the rows from a table to an
           operating system "FLAT FILE".
SQL> SET FEEDBACK OFF
SQL> SET HEADING  OFF
SQL> SET NEWPAGE  0
SQL> SET PAGESIZE 50000
SQL> SPOOL emp_out.dat
SQL> SELECT * FROM EMP ORDER BY EMPNO;
SQL> SPOOL OFF
```

Using The Login.sql File

```
SQL> DEF _EDITOR
DEFINE _EDITOR          = "vi" (CHAR)

Make certain you establish an editor.



SQL> edit login
     SET NUMWIDTH 7
     SET PAGESIZE 24
     DEF _editor=vi
     COL SAL FORMAT $99,999 HEADING 'Monthly|Salary'
     SET UNDERLINE =
     SET PAUSE ON
     SET PAUSE 'Press Return...'
     SET SQLPROMPT "DCI> "
     SET VERIFY   OFF
     SET HEADING  OFF
     SET FEEDBACK OFF
     SELECT 'Good Day......'
     FROM    DUAL;
     SET HEADING  ON
     SET FEEDBACK ON
```

CHAPTER

4

Lunch (Le De´jeuner)

Or

Functions Galore

Common Oracle Functions

NUMBER
ABS
MOD
POWER
ROUND
SQRT

DATE
ADD_MONTHS
LAST_DAY
MONTHS_BETWEEN
NEXT_DAY
TO_CHAR

CHARACTER
INITCAP
INSTR
LENGTH
LOWER
LPAD
RPAD
SUBSTR
UPPER

CONVERSION
LTRIM
SOUNDEX
TO_CHAR
TO_DATE
TO_NUMBER
TRANSLATE
TRUNC

OTHER
DECODE
GREATEST
LEAST
NVL

SINGLE GROUP FUNCTIONS

AVG
COUNT

MAX
MIN
SUM

Using ABS

```
SQL> get cb64
  1   COL      "Days"              FORMAT 99,999
  2   COL       SAL                FORMAT $99,999
  3   COL      "Negative Days"     FORMAT   99,999
  4   SELECT ENAME,
  5     SAL,
  6     TRUNC(ABS(HIREDATE - SYSDATE)) "Days",
  7     TRUNC(HIREDATE     - SYSDATE)  "Negative Days"
  8   FROM    EMP
  9*  ORDER   BY "Days" DESC
SQL> @cb64
```

```
ENAME            SAL     Days Negative Days
----------  --------  ------- -------------
SMITH           $800    5,365        -5,365
ALLEN         $1,600    5,300        -5,300
WARD          $1,250    5,298        -5,298
JONES         $2,975    5,259        -5,259
BLAKE         $2,850    5,230        -5,230
CLARK         $2,450    5,191        -5,191
TURNER        $1,500    5,100        -5,100
MARTIN        $1,250    5,080        -5,080
KING          $5,000    5,030        -5,030
JAMES           $950    5,014        -5,014
FORD          $3,000    5,014        -5,014
MILLER        $1,300    4,963        -4,963
SCOTT         $3,000    4,643        -4,643
ADAMS         $1,100    4,609        -4,609

14 rows selected.
```

Using MOD

How can you create a test table that copies over every third row, assuming employee numbers start with 1 and are incremented by 1, from the EMP table ?

```
SQL> get cb65
  1   CREATE TABLE EMPNO_DIVISIBLE_BY_3 AS
  2          SELECT *
  3          FROM    EMP
  4*         WHERE   MOD(EMPNO, 3) = 0
SQL> /
```

Table created.

```
SQL> SELECT EMPNO, ENAME
  2  FROM    EMPNO_DIVISIBLE_BY_3
  3  ORDER   BY EMPNO;
```

EMPNO ENAME
------- ----------
* 7521 WARD*
* 7566 JONES*
* 7698 BLAKE*
* 7782 CLARK*
* 7788 SCOTT*
* 7839 KING*
* 7902 FORD*

7 rows selected.

Number theory review: If the sum of the digits is a multiple of 3, then the number is a multiple of 3.

WARD: 7 + 5 + 2 + 1 = 15 and 15/3 = 5 with a zero remainder.

JONES:7 + 5 + 6 + 6 = 24 and 24/3 = 8 with a zero remainder.

Using Power

```
SQL> get cb66
  1  COL     "Salary Squared"  FORMAT    $99,999,999
  2  SELECT ENAME,
  3          SAL,
  4          POWER(SAL, 2) "Salary Squared"
  5  FROM    EMP
  6* WHERE   ROWNUM < 3
SQL> @cb66
```

```
ENAME             SAL Salary Squared
---------- -------- --------------
SMITH           $800        $640,000
ALLEN         $1,600      $2,560,000
```

2 rows selected.

```
SQL> SELECT ENAME,
  2          SAL,            -- Nice Try But It Won't Work
  3          SAL ** 2 "Salary Squared"
  4  FROM    EMP
  5  WHERE   ROWNUM < 3;
        SAL ** 2 "Salary Squared"
              *
ERROR at line 3:
ORA-00936: missing expression
```

```
SQL> SHOW SERVEROUTPUT
serveroutput OFF
SQL> SET SERVEROUTPUT ON
SQL> DECLARE
  2      V_MIN_SAL       emp.sal%TYPE;
  3  BEGIN
  4      SELECT min(sal)
  5      INTO   v_min_sal  -- ** Does Work In PL/SQL
  6      FROM   emp;
  7      DBMS_OUTPUT.PUT_LINE(v_min_sal ||
          ' Squared = ' || v_min_sal ** 2);
  8* END;
SQL> /
800 Squared = 640000
PL/SQL procedure successfully completed.
```

Using ROUND

```
SQL> SELECT ROUND(347.864, -3) "-3",
  2          ROUND(347.864, -2) "-2",
  3          ROUND(347.864, -1) "-1",
  4          ROUND(347.864,  0) "0",
  5          ROUND(347.864,  1) "1",
  6          ROUND(347.864,  2) "2",  -- Nearest Hundredth
  7          ROUND(347.864,  3) "3"
  8  FROM    DUAL;
```

-3	-2	-1	0	1	2	3
0	300	350	348	347.9	**347.86**	347.864

1 row selected.

So, if you wish to round off to the nearest penny, then
let the second expression or argument of ROUND be a 2.

Using SQRT

```
SQL> get cb70
  1   COL     ENAME    FORMAT   A6
  2   COL     SAL      FORMAT   9,999
  3   SELECT ENAME,
  4          SAL,
  5          SQRT(SAL) "SQRT OF SAL",
  6          ROUND(SQRT(SAL), 0),
  7          ROUND(SQRT(SAL))
  8   FROM    EMP
  9*  WHERE   ROWNUM < 5
SQL> @cb70
```

ENAME	SAL	SQRT OF SAL	ROUND(SQRT(SAL),0)	ROUND(SQRT(SAL))
SMITH	800	28.2843	28	28
ALLEN	1,600	40	40	40
WARD	1,250	35.3553	35	35
JONES	2,975	54.5436	55	55

Using Last_Day And Next_day

Thanks to my student (Hoa)in Tulsa for asking the following:
When you add new employees, regardless of the actual date
started, you need to show in your employee table their
first day with your company is the FIRST MONDAY of the
following month. Can you do this in Oracle ?

```
SQL> get cb71
  1  SELECT NEXT_DAY(LAST_DAY('&Actual_Date'),'MONDAY') MON
  2* FROM    DUAL
SQL> /
Enter value for actual_date: 27-AUG-95
old 1:SELECT NEXT_DAY(LAST_DAY('&Actual_Date'),'MONDAY') MON
new 1:SELECT NEXT_DAY(LAST_DAY('27-AUG-95'),'MONDAY') MON


MON
---------
04-SEP-95
```

"VERIFY" is set to on so you can better
understand what is occurring. You can also solve this
problem by writing two separate queries.

```
SQL> get cb73
  1  COL     "Last Day Of August Is"  FORMAT  A21
  2  SELECT LAST_DAY('27-AUG-31') "Last Day Of August Is"
  3* FROM    DUAL
SQL> @cb73

Last Day Of August Is
---------------------
31-AUG-31

SQL> SELECT NEXT_DAY('31-AUG-95', 'MONDAY') DOH
  2  FROM    DUAL;

DOH
---------
04-SEP-95
```

> Do you know how many months
> have 28 days?
> Answer: All twelve of them !

Using Add_Months

A customer wants to see the date of the first review,
which occurs six months after the start date, and
not on SAT or SUN.

```
SQL> get cb76
  1   COL     "6 Mos Dy Of Wk"    FORMAT A14
  2   SELECT ENAME, HIREDATE,
  3   DECODE(TO_CHAR(ADD_MONTHS(HIREDATE,6),'DY'), 'SAT',
  4        NEXT_DAY(ADD_MONTHS(HIREDATE,6), 'MONDAY'),
  5                                          'SUN',
  6    NEXT_DAY(ADD_MONTHS(HIREDATE,6), 'MONDAY'),
  7    ADD_MONTHS(HIREDATE,6)) "6 Mon Rev",
  8    ADD_MONTHS(HIREDATE,6) "6 Months",
  9    TO_CHAR(ADD_MONTHS(HIREDATE,6), 'DY') "6 Mos Dy Of Wk"
 10   FROM   EMP
 11* WHERE TO_CHAR(ADD_MONTHS(HIREDATE,6),'DY')  IN('SAT','SUN')
SQL> @cb76
```

```
ENAME        HIREDATE  6 Mon Rev 6 Months  6 Mos Dy Of Wk
---------- --------- --------- --------- --------------
WARD         22-FEB-81 24-AUG-81 22-AUG-81 SAT
MARTIN       28-SEP-81 29-MAR-82 28-MAR-82 SUN
BLAKE        01-MAY-81 02-NOV-81 01-NOV-81 SUN
```

Using Months_Between

If you need months or years an employee has been working at your company, you can use months_between.

```
SQL> get cb77
  1   SELECT ENAME,
  2    HIREDATE,
  3    TRUNC(MONTHS_BETWEEN(SYSDATE,HIREDATE)) "Months",
  4    TRUNC(MONTHS_BETWEEN(SYSDATE,HIREDATE)/12) "Years"
  5   FROM    EMP
  6* ORDER   BY "Years" DESC
SQL> /
```

ENAME	HIREDATE	Months	Years
SMITH	17-DEC-80	176	14
ALLEN	20-FEB-81	174	14
WARD	22-FEB-81	174	14
BLAKE	01-MAY-81	171	14
CLARK	09-JUN-81	170	14
JONES	02-APR-81	172	14
MARTIN	28-SEP-81	166	13
MILLER	23-JAN-82	163	13
FORD	03-DEC-81	164	13
KING	17-NOV-81	165	13
TURNER	08-SEP-81	167	13
JAMES	03-DEC-81	164	13
SCOTT	09-DEC-82	152	12
ADAMS	12-JAN-83	151	12
MCARTHUR	27-AUG-95	0	0

15 rows selected.

Using To_Char To Reformat Dates

Most customers want the date to look like 08/27/95 instead of 27-AUG-95. You can use TO_CHAR, and you can also set your init.ora file parameter NLS_DATE_FORMAT to the format of your liking.

Method 1:
```
SQL> get cb79
  1  COL        DTE       FORMAT  A8
  2  SELECT     ENAME,  TO_CHAR(HIREDATE, 'MM/DD/YY') DTE
  3  FROM       EMP
  4  WHERE      ROWNUM < 5
  5* ORDER      BY HIREDATE DESC;
SQL> @cb79
```

```
ENAME       DTE
----------  --------

JONES       04/02/81
WARD        02/22/81
ALLEN       02/20/81
SMITH       12/17/80
```

Method 2: Legal Dates
```
SQL> get cb80
  1  SELECT TO_CHAR(HIREDATE,
  2  'Day,"the" ddspth "of" Mon,"nineteen-hundred" yysp')
  3  FROM    EMP
  4* WHERE   ROWNUM < 3
SQL> /
```

```
TO_CHAR(HIREDATE,'DAY,"THE"DDSPTH"OF"MON,"NINETEEN-
---------------------------------------------------
Wednesday,the seventeenth of Dec,nineteen-hundred eighty
Friday    ,the twentieth of Feb,nineteen-hundred eighty-one
SQL> SET HEADING OFF
SQL> SELECT TO_CHAR(HIREDATE,
  2  'fmDay,"the" ddspth "of" Mon,"nineteen-hundred" yysp')
  3  FROM    EMP            -- FM Squezzes Data Together
  4* WHERE   ROWNUM < 3;
```

```
Wednesday,the seventeenth of Dec,nineteen-hundred eighty
Friday,the twentieth of Feb,nineteen-hundred eighty-one
```

Using To_Char For Scientific Notation

```
SQL> CREATE TABLE SCIENCE
          (COL1 NUMBER);

Table created.


SQL> INSERT INTO SCIENCE
          VALUES(1.25678E+2);

1 row created.


SQL> SELECT * FROM SCIENCE;

       COL
----------
   125.678


SQL> SELECT TO_CHAR(COL1, '9.99999EEEE')
     FROM    SCIENCE;

TO_CHAR(COL1,
-------------
 1.25678E+02
```

Using To_Char To Reformat Numbers

```
SQL> SELECT  ENAME,
  2          SAL,
  3          TO_CHAR(SAL, '$99,999') "TO_CHAR SAL"
  4* FROM    EMP
SQL> /
```

```
ENAME             SAL  TO_CHAR
----------  ----------  --------
SMITH              800     $800
ALLEN             1600   $1,600
WARD              1250   $1,250
JONES             2975   $2,975
MARTIN            1250   $1,250
BLAKE             2850   $2,850
CLARK             2450   $2,450
SCOTT             3000   $3,000
KING              5000   $5,000
TURNER            1500   $1,500
ADAMS             1100   $1,100
JAMES              950     $950
FORD              3000   $3,000
MILLER            1300   $1,300
MCARTHUR          4100   $4,100

15 rows selected.
```

> Who was it that said, "To be or not to be, that is the
> question?" No, it was not Shakespeare's Hamlet. But, it is
> mathematical. The square root of 4B squared = +2b or -2B.

Determining Number Of Days Until The Year 2000

```
SQL> get cb384
  1  SET     ECHO                OFF
  2  SET     FEEDBACK            OFF
  3  COL     "Days To Yr 2000" FORMAT 99,999
  4  SELECT  TRUNC(TO_DATE('01/01/2000', 'MM/DD/YYYY')
  5          - SYSDATE) "Days To Yr 2000"
  6  FROM    DUAL
  7  /
  8* SET     FEEDBACK            ON
SQL> @cb384


Days To Yr 2000
---------------
          1,567
```

Combining Functions

Thanks be to two U.S. Army students of mine back in 1988 for asking me how they could produce a report with names stored in UPPER CASE that looks like this:
McArthur
Blake

```
SQL> SELECT ENAME,
  2         DECODE(SUBSTR(ENAME,1,2), 'MC',
  3         'Mc' || INITCAP(SUBSTR(ENAME,3,12)),
  4         INITCAP(ENAME)) "US ARMY"
  5  FROM   EMP
  6* ORDER  BY "US ARMY"
SQL> /

ENAME       US ARMY
----------  ----------
ADAMS       Adams
ALLEN       Allen
BLAKE       Blake
CLARK       Clark
FORD        Ford
JAMES       James
JONES       Jones
KING        King
MARTIN      Martin
MCARTHUR    McArthur
MCDONALD    McDonald
MILLER      Miller
SCOTT       Scott
SMITH       Smith
TURNER      Turner
WARD        Ward

16 rows selected.
```

Did you hear about the cross-eyed turtle who tried to kiss an army helmet ?

Using Substr On Rowids

```
SQL> get cb85
  1   COL     "File ID"      FORMAT     A7
  2   SET     SPACE          3
  3   SELECT  ENAME,
  4           ROWID,
  5           SUBSTR(ROWID, 1, 8) "Block",
  6           SUBSTR(ROWID, 10,4) "RSN",
  7           SUBSTR(ROWID, 15,4) "File ID"
  8   FROM    EMP
  9   WHERE   ROWNUM < 5
 10   ORDER   BY ROWID
 11   /
 12*  SET     SPACE          1
SQL> @cb85
```

ENAME	ROWID	Block	RSN	File ID
SMITH	00000A3A.0000.0006	**00000A3A**	**0000**	**0006**
ALLEN	00000A3A.0001.0006	00000A3A	0001	0006
WARD	00000A3A.0002.0006	00000A3A	0002	0006
JONES	00000A3A.0003.0006	00000A3A	0003	0006

4 rows selected.

So, my dear Watson, "SMITH" is in Oracle block 00000A3A, and he is the first row in that block, and he is in file # 6;

If you wanted to see the full path and file name that SMITH is in:

```
SQL> get cb86
  1   COL NAME FORMAT A40
  2   SELECT NAME
  3   FROM   V$DBFILE
  4*  WHERE  FILE# = 6;
SQL> @cb86
```

NAME
/home2/oracle/7.1.3/dbs/USER_data.dbf

Determining The Length Of Data In A Column

I get really, really tired of trying to figure out how wide the data is in a VARCHAR2 column. Here is a tool you can use to make life a little easier.

```
SQL> DESC V$DBFILE
 Name                                  Null?     Type
 ------------------------------------- --------- ----
  FILE#                                          NUMBER
  NAME                                           VARCHAR2(257)


SQL> SELECT MAX(LENGTH(NAME)) "COL NAME FORMAT A??"
  2* FROM    V$DBFILE
SQL> /

COL NAME FORMAT A??
-------------------
                 43
```

Now you do NOT have to guess - you know.

```
SQL> COL NAME FORMAT A43


SQL> SELECT NAME
  2  FROM    V$DBFILE
  3  WHERE   ROWNUM < 5;

NAME
--------------------------------------------
/home2/oracle/7.1.3/dbs/tool2ora713.dbf
/home2/oracle/7.1.3/dbs/USER_data.dbf
/home2/oracle/7.1.3/dbs/USER_idx.dbf
/home2/oracle/7.1.3/dbs/usersora713.dbf
```

Determining Storage Bytes Using Vsize And Length

```
SQL> SELECT ENAME, EMPNO, LENGTH(EMPNO), VSIZE(EMPNO)
  2  FROM    EMP
  3  WHERE   EMPNO = 7900;
```

```
ENAME          EMPNO LENGTH(EMPNO) VSIZE(EMPNO)
---------- ------- ------------- ------------
JAMES           7900             4            2

1 row selected.
```

When it comes to calculating actual storage, VSIZE is much more accurate than LENGTH.

Using Instr

```
SQL> COL "Sun Mon Tue Wed Thu Fri Sat" FORMAT A27
SQL> SELECT ENAME "Last Name",
  2  LPAD('X', INSTR(' SUN MON TUE WED THU FRI SAT',
  3  TO_CHAR(HIREDATE, 'DY'))) "Sun Mon Tue Wed Thu Fri Sat"
  4  FROM       EMP;
```

Last Name	Sun	Mon	Tue	Wed	Thu	Fri	Sat	
SMITH			X					
ALLEN					X			
WARD	X							
JONES				X				
MARTIN		X						
BLAKE						**X**		Notice Blake hired
CLARK		X						*on Friday.*
SCOTT				X				
KING		X						
TURNER		X						
ADAMS			X					
JAMES				X				
FORD				X				
MILLER						X		
MCARTHUR	X							
MCDONALD								

```
16 rows selected.

SQL> get cb90
  1  COL     "Day Of Wk"    FORMAT    A9
  2  SELECT ENAME,
  3          TO_CHAR(HIREDATE, 'DY') "Day Of Wk"
  4  FROM    EMP
  5* WHERE   ENAME = 'BLAKE'
SQL> @cb90
```

ENAME	Day Of Wk
BLAKE	**FRI**

Mailing Labels Using Rpad

```
SQL> COL NAME   FORMAT A12
SQL> COL ADDR1  FORMAT A18
SQL> COL ADDR2  FORMAT A9
SQL> COL CITY   FORMAT A10
SQL> SELECT *
  2* FROM   ADDRESS;

NAME          ADDR1               ADDR2      CITY        ST ZIP
------------  ------------------  ---------  ----------  -- -----
DEBRA PAIGE   222 FANTASIA        BOX 97509  SAN ANTONIO TX 75222
CHEF PIERRE   2300 COLLEEN COURT             CARROLLTON  TX 75007
SAUL          WITNESS LANE                   TARSUS      IS 11111

SQL> get cb387
  1   SET     HEADING   OFF
  2   SET     FEEDBACK  OFF
  3   SET     LINESIZE  40
  4   SELECT RPAD(NAME, 40),
  5          RPAD(ADDR1,40),
  6          RPAD(DECODE(ADDR2,NULL,CITY || ', ' || STATE, ADDR2), 40),
  7          RPAD(DECODE(ADDR2,NULL,ZIP,CITY || ', ' || STATE),   40),
  8          RPAD(DECODE(ADDR2,NULL,'   ',ZIP),                   40)
  9   FROM   ADDRESS;
 10   SET     HEADING   ON
 11   SET     FEEDBACK  ON
 12*  SET     LINESIZE  80
SQL> @cb387

DEBRA PAIGE
222 FANTASIA
BOX 97509
SAN ANTONIO, TX
75222

CHEF PIERRE
2300 COLLEEN COURT
CARROLLTON, TX
75007


SAUL
WITNESS LANE
TARSUS, IS
11111
```

Formatting Dates Using To_date

If you want to use your own date format instead of Oracle's, use TO_DATE to inform Oracle just exactly what is meant by each character in your date string. Also, as a performance note, if there is any chance for the RULE or COST optimizers to use an index, place the TO_DATE on the string and NOT on the column. If placed on the column, Oracle performs a full table scan.

```
SQL> SELECT ENAME, HIREDATE
  2  FROM    EMP
  3  WHERE   HIREDATE > TO_DATE('12/11/81', 'MM/DD/YY');

ENAME      HIREDATE
---------- ---------
SCOTT      09-DEC-82
ADAMS      12-JAN-83
MILLER     23-JAN-82
MCARTHUR   27-AUG-95
```

As an Oracle employee from 03-MAY-88 through 15-AUG-93, I traveled very extensively, and would often stop in our local grocery store to cash a check so I would have some spending money for food etc. I always use the Oracle date format on our checks. Several times, the part-time high school or college student would say, "What a weird way to write the date". I would reply with my chest puffed out, "You don't understand,--- I work for Oracle". To which they countered, "You don't understand,--- I work for Kroger".

Formatting Dates Using NLS_DATE_FORMAT

<u>INIT.ORA</u>

NLS_DATE_FORMAT = "YYYY-MM-DD HH24:MI:SS"

Given the above, you have at least two different means of
retrieving all employees hired after 09/16/96.

```
SQL> SELECT *
  2  FROM    EMP
  3* WHERE   HIREDATE > '1995-09-16 00:00:00'
```

```
SQL> SELECT *
  2  FROM    EMP
  3  WHERE   HIREDATE >
  4*         TO_DATE('16-SEP-95','DD-MON-YY')
```

WARNING: Setting nls_date_format in the parameter file
impacts all applications and users in your database. Scripts
written before you made this error out if the script is
inserting or updating a DATE column.

```
What do you call 5 French Cats on thin ice ?
Un, Du, Twa, Kat, Canq
```

Formatting License Plates Using Soundex

	Returns
`SQL> SELECT SOUNDEX('CAROLE') FROM DUAL;`	*C640*
`SQL> SELECT SOUNDEX('PAIGE') FROM DUAL;`	*P200*
`SQL> SELECT SOUNDEX('DEBRA') FROM DUAL;`	*D160*
`SQL> SELECT SOUNDEX('KERRY') FROM DUAL;`	*K600*
`SQL> SELECT SOUNDEX('KEVIN') FROM DUAL;`	*K150*
`SQL> SELECT SOUNDEX('KATHY') FROM DUAL;`	*K300*
`SQL> SELECT SOUNDEX('STAN') FROM DUAL;`	*S350*
`SQL> SELECT SOUNDEX('PIERRE') FROM DUAL;`	*P600*

I have been told soundex is used for license plates. Hope nobody I know ever has to make any!

SOUNDEX CODING GUIDE

```
The number     Represents the letters
    1              B P F V
    2              C S K G J Q X Z
    3              D T
    4              L
    5              M N
    6              R
```

Disregard the letters A, E, I, O, U, W, Y, and H.

Every SOUNDEX CODE contains 4 characters, one letter followed by three numbers. The letter is always the first letter of the surname. Disregard vowels after the first letter of the surname, and if there are not 3 consonants, use zeros to plug the three-digit code.

NAMES WITH PREFIXES
Code it both with and without the prefix.

NAMES WITH DOUBLE LETTERS
Treat double letters as one letter. i.e. PIERRE you would cross out the second R.

NAMES WITH LETTERS NEXT TO EACH OTHER WITH THE SAME #
Treat them as one letter.
JACKSON CK and S have a code of 2. Throw out K and S.

Identifying "%" In Columns Using Translate

There was a customer in Houston, who seemed at least
seven feet tall, who said he was not leaving my class until
I showed him how to identify all rows containing a
percent sign % in a particular column. He was not a happy
camper.

So, to simulate the problem, I inserted DEB%A into EMP.

```
SQL> INSERT INTO EMP(EMPNO,ENAME,DEPTNO,JOB,SAL)
  2   VALUES(7777,'DEB%A',10,'ACTRESS',5500);
```

1 row created.

```
SQL> SELECT ENAME
  2  FROM    EMP
  3  WHERE   TRANSLATE(ENAME, '%', '!') LIKE '%!%';
```

ENAME

DEB%A

You are asking Oracle to look at the data in the ENAME
column looking for a per cent sign(%). And, for every
one found, translate the "%" into a "!". The
purpose of the "LIKE" is to determine if there are any
translations, and if there are, return the row.

After I wrote this, and showed it to him, he smiled like he
just ate a possum.

> *When on the island of Oahu, Hawaii be*
> *very careful how you pronounce the name of*
> **"LIKE LIKE".**

Validating Social Security Format Using Translate

Look at SSN and translate all numbers to a "9" and all
dashes "-" to a dash "-".

```
SQL> ALTER TABLE EMP
  2        ADD    SSN CHAR(11);
```

Table altered.

```
SQL> ALTER   TABLE        EMP
  2   ADD    CONSTRAINT   CK_EMP_SSN
  3   CHECK(TRANSLATE(SSN,'0123456789-',
  4                       '9999999999-') = '999-99-9999');
```

Table altered.

```
SQL> UPDATE EMP
  2        SET SSN = '2605-9-1234'
  3        WHERE EMPNO = 7902;
       WHERE EMPNO = 7902
                        *
ERROR at line 3:
ORA-02290: check constraint (STUDENT15.CK_EMP_SSN) violated

SQL> 1
  1  UPDATE EMP
  2        SET SSN = '260-59-1234'
  3*       WHERE EMPNO = 7902
SQL> /
```

1 row updated.

```
SQL> SELECT ENAME,
  2        SSN
  3  FROM   EMP
  4  WHERE  SSN IS NOT NULL;
ENAME      SSN
---------- -----------
FORD       260-59-1234
```

Validating Field/Item Formats Using Translate

SQL*Forms V3.0

ON-VALIDATE-FIELD Trigger On SSN Field

```
IF TRANSLATE(:EMP.SSN, '0123456789-', '9999999999-')
   <> '999-99-9999'
   THEN
   MESSAGE('Valid SSN Format Is 999-99-9999');
   RAISE FORM_TRIGGER_FAILURE;
END IF;
```

Oracle Forms 4.0 And 4.5

WHEN-VALIDATE-ITEM

Same code as above.

Preventing Nulls From Appearing In Totals Using NVL

```
SQL> SELECT  ENAME,
  2          SAL,
  3          COMM,
  4          SAL + COMM "Tot Mon Salary"
  5  FROM    EMP
  6  WHERE   ROWNUM < 5;
```

```
ENAME           SAL     COMM Tot Mon Salary
---------- ------- ------- --------------
SMITH           800
ALLEN          1600      300           1900
WARD           1250      500           1750
JONES          2975
```

4 rows selected.

Bertha and Ernest are not happy about the far right column in the report. They want to see 800 for SMITH etc.

```
SQL> COL "Tot Mon Salary" FORMAT $99,999
SQL> SELECT  ENAME,
  2          SAL,
  3          COMM,
  4          NVL(SAL,0) + NVL(COMM,0) "Tot Mon Salary"
  5  FROM    EMP
  6* WHERE   ROWNUM < 5
SQL> /
```

```
ENAME           SAL     COMM Tot Mon Salary
---------- ------- ------- --------------
SMITH           800                    $800
ALLEN          1600      300         $1,900
WARD           1250      500         $1,750
JONES          2975                 $2,975
```

NVL Used With Other Functions

```
SQL> SELECT MAX(DEPTNO) FROM DEPT;

MAX(DEPTNO)
-----------
         99

SQL> SELECT COUNT(*)  -- Will ALWAYS Return A Number
  2  FROM    DEPT
  3* WHERE   DEPTNO = 1234;

COUNT(*)
--------
       0

SQL> SELECT NVL(MAX(DEPTNO),0) + 1
  2* FROM    DEPT;

NVL(MAX(DEPTNO),0)+1
--------------------
                 100


SQL> SELECT NVL(MAX(DEPTNO),0) + 1
  2  FROM    DEPT
  3* WHERE   DEPTNO = 9876;


NVL(MAX(DEPTNO),0)+1
--------------------
                   1
```

So, even though there is no department 9876 in the DEPT table, the function MAX returns a number or a NULL. In this case, a NULL is returned since there is no match on the "WHERE" clause. However, since NVL is applied to whatever MAX returns, the NULL becomes a zero. Then, one is added to the zero to return a 1.

This concept is utilized in forms whenever you want to sequence line items. Sequences are used on the primary key columns, and the above code can be used on non primary key columns.

Analyzing Bonus Projections Using Decode

Say you are thinking about giving all employees in
department 10 a 20% bonus, department 20 15%, and
everyone else does not receive a bonus.

```
SQL> SET     FEEDBACK      OFF
  2  BREAK   ON   DEPTNO   SKIP   1
  3  COL   "SAL" FORMAT   $99,990    HEADING 'Mo Sal'
  4  COL      "Bonus"      FORMAT      $99,990
  5  COMPUTE SUM          OF "SAL"    ON DEPTNO
  6  COMPUTE SUM          OF "Bonus" ON DEPTNO
  7  SELECT DEPTNO, ENAME, NVL(SAL,0) "SAL",
  8         DECODE(DEPTNO,10, .2  * NVL(SAL,0),
  9                       20, .15 * NVL(SAL,0),
 10                                0) "Bonus"
 11  FROM    EMP
 12  WHERE   DEPTNO IN(10,20) OR ENAME = 'BLAKE'
 13  ORDER   BY DEPTNO, "Bonus" DESC;
 14  SET     FEEDBACK      ON
 15  CLEAR BREAKS COMPUTES
SQL> @cb108
DEPTNO ENAME          Mo Sal      Bonus
------- ----------   --------   --------

    10 DEB%A          $5,500     $1,100     20% OF $5,500=$1,100
       KING           $5,000     $1,000
       MCARTHUR       $4,100       $820
       CLARK          $2,450       $490
       MILLER         $1,300       $260
       MCDONALD           $0         $0
*******                --------   --------
sum                   $18,350     $3,670


    20 SCOTT          $3,000       $450     15% OF $3,000=$450
       FORD           $3,000       $450
       JONES          $2,975       $446
       ADAMS          $1,100       $165
       SMITH            $800       $120
*******                --------   --------
sum                   $10,875     $1,631


    30 BLAKE          $2,850         $0     NO BONUS FOR DEPT 30
*******                --------   --------
sum                    $2,850         $0
```

Preventing Division By Zero Using Decode

```
SQL> get cb109
  1   COL     "Sal/Comm Ratio"   FORMAT   A9
  2   SET     SPACE          5
  3   SELECT ENAME,
  4          SAL,
  5          COMM,
  6          DECODE(COMM, 0, 'comm is 0',
  7                  NULL, 'null comm',
  8                  TRUNC(SAL/COMM, 2)) "Sal/Comm Ratio"
  9   FROM    EMP
 10   /
 11*  SET     SPACE          1

SQL> @cb109
```

ENAME	SAL	COMM	Sal/Comm
SMITH	800		null comm
ALLEN	1600	300	5.33
WARD	1250	500	2.5
JONES	2975		null comm
MARTIN	1250	1400	.89
BLAKE	2850		null comm
CLARK	2450		null comm
SCOTT	3000		null comm
KING	5000		null comm
TURNER	1500	0	comm is 0
ADAMS	1100		null comm
JAMES	950		null comm
FORD	3000		null comm
MILLER	1300		null comm
MCARTHUR	4100		null comm
MCDONALD			null comm
DEB%A	5500		null comm

17 rows selected.

Quarterly Report Using Decode

```
SQL> get cb110
  1  SET        FEEDBACK               OFF
  2  BREAK                             ON REPORT
  3  COMPUTE    SUM   OF  QTR1         ON   REPORT
  4  COMPUTE    SUM   OF  QTR2         ON   REPORT
  5  COMPUTE    SUM   OF  QTR3         ON   REPORT
  6  COMPUTE    SUM   OF  QTR4         ON   REPORT
  7  COMPUTE    SUM   OF  TOT_BY_YR    ON   REPORT
  8  COL        QTR1                   FORMAT      $999,990
  9  COL        QTR2                   FORMAT      $999,990
 10  COL        QTR3                   FORMAT      $999,990
 11  COL        QTR4                   FORMAT      $999,990
 12  COL        TOT_BY_YR              FORMAT      $999,990
 13  COL        "YEAR"                 FORMAT      A4
 14  SELECT TO_CHAR(HIREDATE, 'YYYY') "YEAR",
 15  SUM(DECODE(TO_CHAR(HIREDATE,'MON'),
 16             'JAN',sal,'FEB',sal,'MAR',sal,0)) QTR1,
 17  SUM(DECODE(TO_CHAR(HIREDATE,'MON'),
 18             'APR',sal,'MAY',sal,'JUN',sal,0)) QTR2,
 19  SUM(DECODE(TO_CHAR(HIREDATE,'MON'),
 20             'JUL',sal,'AUG',sal,'SEP',sal,0)) QTR3,
 21  SUM(DECODE(TO_CHAR(HIREDATE,'MON'),
 22             'OCT',sal,'NOV',sal,'DEC',sal,0)) QTR4,
 23  SUM(SAL) TOT_BY_YR
 24  FROM       EMP
 25  GROUP      BY TO_CHAR(HIREDATE, 'YYYY');
 26  SET        FEEDBACK               ON
 27  CLEAR      BREAKS
 28  CLEAR      COMPUTES
 29* CLEAR      COLUMNS

SQL> @cb110
```

YEAR	QTR1	QTR2	QTR3	QTR4	TOT_BY_YR
1980	$0	$0	$0	$800	$800
1981	$2,850	$8,275	$2,750	$8,950	$22,825
1982	$1,300	$0	$0	$3,000	$4,300
1983	$1,100	$0	$0	$0	$1,100
1995	$0	$0	$9,600	$0	$9,600
sum	$5,250	$8,275	$12,350	$12,750	$38,625

Matrix Report Using Decode

```
SQL> get cb115
  1  SELECT
  2  SUM(DECODE(TO_CHAR(HIREDATE, 'DY'), 'MON', 1, 0)) "MON"
  3* FROM EMP
SQL> /


       MON
----------
         1
```

Pretend there is a bucket labeled MON, and if an
employee is hired on a Monday (MON), toss a 1
into the MON bucket. If the employee is not hired on a
Monday, then toss a 0(zero)in the MON bucket
to be SUMed with whatever the running total is. The trick
here is the column alias.

```
SQL> get cb116
  1  SELECT
  2  SUM(DECODE(TO_CHAR(HIREDATE,'DY'), 'MON', 1, 0)) "MON",
  3  SUM(DECODE(TO_CHAR(HIREDATE,'DY'), 'TUE', 1, 0)) "TUE"
  4* FROM EMP
SQL> /


       MON        TUE
---------- ----------
         1          2
```

```
SQL> SELECT
  2  SUM(DECODE(TO_CHAR(HIREDATE,'DY'), 'MON', 1, 0)) "MON",
  3  SUM(DECODE(TO_CHAR(HIREDATE,'DY'), 'TUE', 1, 0)) "TUE",
  4  SUM(DECODE(TO_CHAR(HIREDATE,'DY'), 'WED', 1, 0)) "WED",
  5  SUM(DECODE(TO_CHAR(HIREDATE,'DY'), 'THU', 1, 0)) "THU",
  6  SUM(DECODE(TO_CHAR(HIREDATE,'DY'), 'FRI', 1, 0)) "FRI",
  7  SUM(DECODE(TO_CHAR(HIREDATE,'DY'), 'SAT', 1, 0)) "SAT",
  8  SUM(DECODE(TO_CHAR(HIREDATE,'DY'), 'SUN', 1, 0)) "SUN"
  9* FROM EMP
SQL> /
```

MON	TUE	WED	THU	FRI	SAT	SUN
1	2	2	7	1	1	3

Simple Matrix Report Using Count

```
SQL> get cb118
  1   SET      SPACE           6
  2   COL      "Day Hired"    FORMAT    A9
  3   SELECT TO_CHAR(HIREDATE, 'DY') "Day Hired",
  4          COUNT(*) "# Hired This Day"
  5   FROM     EMP
  6   GROUP  BY TO_CHAR(HIREDATE, 'DY')
  7   /
  8*  SET      SPACE           1


SQL> @cb118

Day Hired      # Hired This Day
---------      ----------------
FRI                           1
MON                           1
SAT                           1
SUN                           3
THU                           7
TUE                           2
WED                           2

7 rows selected.
```

Another Matrix Report Using Decode

```
SQL> get cb140
  1   TTITLE 'Matrix Jobs By Department'
  2   BREAK                              ON REPORT
  3   COMPUTE SUM OF "10"                ON REPORT
  4   COMPUTE SUM OF "20"                ON REPORT
  5   COMPUTE SUM OF "30"                ON REPORT
  6   COMPUTE SUM OF "TOTAL_BY_JOB" ON REPORT
  7   SELECT JOB,
  8          SUM(DECODE(DEPTNO, 10, 1, 0)) "10",
  9          SUM(DECODE(DEPTNO, 20, 1, 0)) "20",
 10          SUM(DECODE(DEPTNO, 30, 1, 0)) "30",
 11          COUNT(*) "TOTAL_BY_JOB"
 12   FROM    EMP
 13   GROUP   BY JOB;
 14   TTITLE OFF
 15*  CLEAR   BREAKS
SQL> @cb140
```

Wed Aug 30   page   1
                      Matrix Jobs By Department

JOB	10	20	30	TOTAL_BY_JOB
ANALYST	0	2	0	2
CLERK	1	2	1	4
MANAGER	1	1	1	3
PRESIDENT	1	0	0	1
SALESMAN	0	0	4	4
	-------	-------	-------	------------
sum	3	5	6	14

Equal Range Reporting Using Decode

Thanks to the folks in Richmond, Virginia for asking me to do this for them.

They wanted to recognize all employees that had worked for their company (govt) 5 years, 10 years, 15 years, and so on. So, we are talking about EQUAL RANGES.

Lets look at one employee, and look at his length of service, and see if the number of months falls between 60 months (5 years) and less than 120 months.

Three possibilities exist.

Possibility one: Employee has less than 5 years of service.
                    Say 56 months.
                    GREATEST(60, 56)   = 60
                    LEAST(119, 56)   = 56
                    Since 60 does not equal 56, the employee does not fall into this category.

Possibility two: Employee has more than 5 years of service.
                    Say 126 months. (10 1/2 years)
                    GREATEST(60, 126) = 126
                    LEAST(119, 126)   = 119
                    Once again, the numbers are different indicating this employee does not fit into this range.

Possibility three: Employee has worked more than 5 years and less than 10 years.
                    Say 65 months. (5 years and 5 months)
                    GREATEST(60, 65)   = 65
                    LEAST(119, 65)   = 65
                    This time the numbers match indicating the employee's length of service falls in the range of greater than 5 years, and less than 10 years.

(Continued)

By comparing the length of service in months to the minimum number of months in our range, say 65 months of actual service to 50 months, and returning the GREATEST of the two, you have 65. And, comparing 65 months to the maximum number of months in your range, 65 months to 119 months, and returning the LEAST of the two, you have 65 again which indicates the length of service falls between 60 months and 119 months.

On the REAL NUMBER LINE it looks like this:
```
-119          -60          0          +60 x          +119
```
Here, "X" marks the spot of 65 months.

Mathematically speaking, any real number x is said to be in the range between 60 and 119, if and only if, $x \geq 60$ AND $x \leq 119$. Or put another way, **60 <= x <= 119.** In Oracle, you compare 65 to the minimum of this range 60, and see which number is the larger or greater. Hence, **GREATEST(60, 65) = 65.**

Then, you compare 65 to the maximum of this range 119, and see which number is the smaller or least.
Hence, **LEAST(65, 119) = 65.**
Obviously, since the numbers are the same, the number 65 is between 60 and 119.

```
SQL> get cb119
  1   SELECT ENAME,
  2          HIREDATE,
  3   DECODE(GREATEST(60,TRUNC(MONTHS_BETWEEN(
  4          SYSDATE,HIREDATE))),
  5          LEAST(119,TRUNC(MONTHS_BETWEEN(
  6          SYSDATE,HIREDATE))), '5 YR AWARD') "Award"
  7*  FROM   EMP
SQL> /
ENAME       HIREDATE  Award
----------  --------- ----------
SMITH       17-DEC-80
ALLEN       20-FEB-81
WARD        22-AUG-85
JONES       02-APR-81
MARTIN      28-SEP-81
BLAKE       23-AUG-90 5 YR AWARD
CLARK       09-JUN-81
SCOTT       09-DEC-82
KING        23-AUG-90 5 YR AWARD
```

Correcting Error ORA-00937

Say you want to see the department number, and the number of employees in each department.

```
SQL> SELECT DEPTNO,
  2          COUNT(*) "# Emps By Dept"
  3  FROM    EMP;
SELECT DEPTNO,
        *
ERROR at line 1:
ORA-00937: not a single-group group function
```

Since SQL cannot return many department numbers, and one row of a count simultaneously, in this particular case, you need to add the **GROUP BY clause.**

```
SQL> L
  1  SELECT DEPTNO,
  2          COUNT(*) "# Emps By Dept"
  3  FROM    EMP
  4* GROUP   BY DEPTNO
SQL> /

    DEPTNO # Emps By Dept
---------- --------------
        10              6
        20              5
        30              6
```

Another Method Of Correcting Error ORA-00937

However, you don't always use the GROUP BY clause to solve this problem. What if you want to see the most senior employee with respect to length of service. You might be lulled into writing:

```
SQL> SELECT ENAME, MIN(HIREDATE)
  2  FROM    EMP;
SELECT ENAME, MIN(HIREDATE)
       *
ERROR at line 1:
ORA-00937: not a single-group group function
```

And, if you try the following, you merely return the entire table:

```
SQL> L
  1  SELECT ENAME, MIN(HIREDATE)
  2  FROM    EMP
  3* GROUP   BY ENAME
SQL> /
```

In this case, you can either write two separate queries, or write a subquery.

```
SQL> SELECT ENAME, HIREDATE
  2  FROM    EMP
  3  WHERE   HIREDATE = (SELECT MIN(HIREDATE)
  4                      FROM    EMP);


ENAME      HIREDATE
---------- ---------
SMITH      17-DEC-80
```

Identifying Duplicate Primary Keys

```
SQL> GET cons
  1  SET     VERIFY    OFF
  2  COL     CONSTRAINT_NAME         FORMAT    A14
  3  COL     CONSTRAINT_TYPE         HEADING TYPE  FORMAT A4
  4  COL     SEARCH_CONDITION        FORMAT    A25
  5  SELECT CONSTRAINT_NAME,
  6          CONSTRAINT_TYPE,
  7          SEARCH_CONDITION
  8  FROM    USER_CONSTRAINTS
  9* WHERE   TABLE_NAME = UPPER('&Table')
SQL> @cons
Enter value for table: emp

CONSTRAINT_NAM TYPE SEARCH_CONDITION
-------------- ---- -------------------------
SYS_C006893    C    EMPNO IS NOT NULL
```

Notice, the primary key constraint is disabled, or it is dropped, or it never existed in the first place.

```
SQL> UPDATE EMP SET EMPNO = 7902 WHERE ROWNUM < 5;

4 rows updated.
```

Deliberately produced duplicate employee numbers.

```
SQL> get add_pk
  1  ALTER TABLE EMP
  2      ADD   CONSTRAINT  PK_EMP_EMPNO
  3      PRIMARY KEY(EMPNO)
  4      USING INDEX
  5      TABLESPACE USER_INDEX
  6*      STORAGE(INITIAL 2K   NEXT 2K)
SQL> /
ALTER TABLE EMP
*
ERROR at line 1:
ORA-02299: cannot add or enable constraint
(STUDENT15.PK_EMP_EMPNO)-duplicate keys found
```

Another Method To Identify Duplicate Primary Keys

*Method 1: Using **HAVING***
```
SQL> SELECT  EMPNO, COUNT(*)
  2  FROM    EMP
  3  GROUP   BY       EMPNO
  4* HAVING COUNT(*)  > 1;

  EMPNO COUNT(*)
 ------- --------
   7902        5

SQL> SELECT  EMPNO, ROWID, ENAME
  2  FROM    EMP
  3  WHERE   EMPNO  =  7902;

  EMPNO ROWID               ENAME
 ------- ------------------- ----------
   7902 0000025D.0000.0006 SMITH
   7902 0000025D.0001.0006 ALLEN
   7902 0000025D.0002.0006 WARD
   7902 0000025D.0003.0006 JONES
   7902 0000025D.000C.0006 FORD
```

You can delete or update SMITH, ALLEN, WARD and JONES
using their ROWID's. Or, you can use a CORRELATED DELETE
which is extremely slow on large tables. So, to keep FORD,
and delete SMITH, ALLEN, WARD, and JONES:

```
SQL> DELETE FROM EMP X
  2          WHERE    X.ROWID < (SELECT MAX(ROWID)
  3                              FROM    EMP
  4                              WHERE   X.EMPNO = EMP.EMPNO);

4 rows deleted.

SQL> SELECT ROWID, EMPNO, ENAME FROM EMP WHERE EMPNO = 7902;

ROWID                EMPNO ENAME
------------------- ------- ----------
0000025D.000C.0006    7902 FORD
```

Still Another Method To Identify Duplicate Primary Keys

*Method 2: Using the **EXCEPTIONS** table*

SQL> get $ORACLE_HOME/rdbms/admin/utlexcpt
SQL> rem $Header: utlexcpt.sql 7001200.1 92/11/03 17:30:27
twang Generic<base> $

I removed several lines from this script. Just comments.

SQL> Rem Copyright (c) 1991 by Oracle Corporation
SQL> Rem   NAME
SQL> Rem   MODIFIED   (MM/DD/YY)
SQL> Rem glumpkin   10/20/92 - Renamed from EXCEPT.SQL

SQL> create table exceptions(row_id rowid,
* 2   owner varchar2(30),*
* 3   table_name varchar2(30),*
* 4   constraint varchar2(30));*
Table created.

SQL> ALTER TABLE EMP ADD CONSTRAINT PK_EMP_EMPNO
** 2   PRIMARY KEY(EMPNO) USING INDEX**
** 3   TABLESPACE USER_INDEX**
** 4   STORAGE(INITIAL 4K   NEXT 4K)**
** 5   EXCEPTIONS INTO EXCEPTIONS;**
ALTER TABLE EMP
*
ERROR at line 1:
ORA-02299: cannot add or enable constraint
(STUDENT15.PK_EMP_EMPNO)- duplicate
keys found

Who was that masked man? To see who the culprits are:
SQL> SELECT EMPNO, ENAME
** 2 FROM   EMP,   EXCEPTIONS X**
** 3 WHERE EMP.ROWID = X.ROW_ID;**
EMPNO ENAME
------- ----------
*   7902 SMITH*
*   7902 ALLEN*
*   **7902 FORD**   Ford is ok.*
*   7902 WARD*
*   7902 JONES*

CHAPTER

5

After Lunch Snack (Le Gouter) Or Database Links, Indexes, Sequences, Snapshots, Synonyms, Tables, And Views

Creating A Database Link

```
> sqlplus system/manager

SQL> CREATE      DATABASE LINK ORA716  /* LINK 713 TO 716 */
     CONNECT     TO STUDENT15   -- SQL*Net V2
     IDENTIFIED BY STUDENT15 /*t=tcp node=dci2 sid=ORA716*/
     USING 't:dci2:ORA716';
Link created.

SQL> SELECT * FROM V$DATABASE;
```

NAME	CREATED	LOG_MODE	CHECKPOINT_ CHANGE#	ARCHIVE_ CHANGE#
ORA713	12/27/94 14:56:27	NOARCHIVELOG	255444	255394

```
SQL> host env | grep ORACLE_SID
ORACLE_SID=ora713

SQL> SELECT SUBSTR(OWNER,    1,  6) "Owner",
            SUBSTR(DB_LINK,  1, 12) "DB_Link",
            SUBSTR(USERNAME, 1,  9) "Username",
            SUBSTR(HOST,     1, 13) "Host",
            CREATED "Created"
     FROM   SYS.DBA_LINKS;
```

Owner	DB_Link	Username	Host	Created
SYSTEM	ORA716.WORLD	STUDENT15	t:dci2:ORA716	04-AUG-95

```
SQL> SHOW USER
user is "SYSTEM"

SQL> CONNECT STUDENT15/STUDENT15@t:dci2:ORA716
Connected.

SQL> SELECT * FROM V$DATABASE;
```

NAME	CREATED	LOG_MODE	CHECKPOINT_ CHANGE#	ARCHIVE_ CHANGE#
ORA716	06/15/94 17:41:30	NOARCHIVELOG	258389	257387

Using A Database Link

```
SQL> CREATE TABLE DRIVERS
           (DNO         NUMBER,
            CAR_NO      VARCHAR2(3),
            DNAME       VARCHAR2(20))
     TABLESPACE   USER_DATA;
Table created.
SQL> INSERT INTO DRIVERS VALUES(200, '99', 'LEE WALLARD');
1 row created.
SQL> COL CAR_NO FORMAT A6
SQL> SELECT * FROM DRIVERS;
DNO     CAR_NO DNAME
------  ------ --------------------
200     99     LEE WALLARD

SQL> SHOW USER
user is "STUDENT15"
SQL> EXIT

> sqlplus system/manager

SQL> SELECT * FROM GLOBAL_NAME;

GLOBAL_NAME
---------------
ORA713.WORLD

SQL> SELECT *        /*  ONE WAY TO USE THE LINK  */
     FROM   STUDENT15.DRIVERS@ORA716;

DNO     CAR_NO DNAME
------  ------ --------------------
200     99     LEE WALLARD

SQL> CREATE PUBLIC SYNONYM  /*  LOCATION TRANSPARENCY  */
          DRIVERS FOR STUDENT15.DRIVERS@ORA716;
Synonym created.

SQL> SELECT * FROM DRIVERS;
DNO     CAR_NO DNAME
------  ------ --------------------
200     99     LEE WALLARD
```

Creating Unique Indexes On The Primary Key

Method 1: Create Table Command
First of all, you want your indexes in one tablespace on
one disk drive, and your table data in another tablespace.

```
SQL> SELECT TABLESPACE_NAME
  2* FROM   SYS.DBA_TABLESPACES;
TABLESPACE_NAME
--------------------------------
SYSTEM
RBS
TEMP
TOOLS
USERS
USER_DATA
USER_INDEX
7 rows selected.

SQL> CREATE TABLE       IOUW
  2           (ID       NUMBER(6,0),
  3            CNAME    VARCHAR2(30),
  4            CITY     VARCHAR2(20),
  5            STATE    CHAR(2),
  6            PHONE    VARCHAR2(15),
  7            RDATE    DATE,
  8            CONSTRAINT  PK_IOUW
  9            PRIMARY  KEY(ID)
 10            USING    INDEX
 11                     TABLESPACE USER_INDEX
 12                     STORAGE(INITIAL 4K  NEXT 4K))
 13  TABLESPACE         USER_DATA
 14*                    STORAGE(INITIAL 4K  NEXT 4K);
Table created.

SQL> SELECT INDEX_NAME, TABLESPACE_NAME, UNIQUENESS
  4  FROM   SYS.DBA_INDEXES
  5  WHERE  OWNER = UPPER('&Owner') AND
  6*        TABLE_NAME = UPPER('&Table');

Enter value for owner: STUDENT15
Enter value for table: IOUW
INDEX_NAME          TABLESPACE_NAME        UNIQUENES
----------          ---------------        ---------
    PK_IOUW             USER_INDEX             UNIQUE
```

Another Way To Create Unique Indexes On Primary Key

Method 2:   Alter Table Add Constraint

```
SQL> DROP INDEX PK_IOUW;
DROP INDEX PK_IOUW
*
ERROR at line 1:
ORA-02429: cannot drop index used for enforcement of
unique/primary key
 SQL> ALTER TABLE IOUW
   2         DROP CONSTRAINT PK_IOUW;
Table altered.
SQL> get are
   1  SELECT INDEX_NAME,
   2         TABLESPACE_NAME,
   3         UNIQUENESS
   4  FROM    SYS.DBA_INDEXES
   5  WHERE   OWNER = UPPER('&Owner') AND
   6*         TABLE_NAME = UPPER('&Table')
SQL> /
Enter value for owner: STUDENT15
Enter value for table: IOUW

no rows selected
SQL> -- No Rows Selected Means The Table Has No Indexes

SQL> L
   1  ALTER    TABLE    IOUW
   2           ADD      CONSTRAINT PK_IOUW
   3           PRIMARY KEY(ID)
   4           USING    INDEX
   5                    TABLESPACE USER_INDEX
   6*         STORAGE(INITIAL 4K   NEXT 4K)
SQL> /
Table altered.

SQL> @are
Enter value for owner: STUDENT15
Enter value for table: IOUW

INDEX_NAME        TABLESPACE_NAME        UNIQUENES
----------        ---------------        ---------
    PK_IOUW           USER_INDEX             UNIQUE
```

Still Another Way To Create Unique Indexes On PK's

Method 3:   Alter Table Enable Constraint

```
SQL> ALTER  TABLE  IOUW
  2          DISABLE CONSTRAINT PK_IOUW;
Table altered.
```

```
SQL> @are
Enter value for owner: student15
Enter value for table: iouw
```

no rows selected

In other words, when you disable a primary key constraint,
the primary key (UNIQUE) index gets **DROPPED !!**

```
SQL> ALTER  TABLE  IOUW
  2*         ENABLE CONSTRAINT PK_IOUW;
```

Table altered.

```
SQL> @are
Enter value for owner: student15
Enter value for table: iouw
```

INDEX_NAME	TABLESPACE_NAME	UNIQUENES
PK_IOUW	**USER_DATA**	UNIQUE

It follows when you enable a primary key constraint,
the primary key(UNIQUE) index gets re-created. However,
if you do not specify the tablespace for the unique index,
it defaults to the same tablespace as the table data which
leads to contention on the disk.

```
SQL> ALTER TABLE IOUW
  2        ENABLE CONSTRAINT PK_IOUW
  3        USING  INDEX
  4             TABLESPACE USER_INDEX
  5             STORAGE(INITIAL 4K  NEXT 4K);
```

Table altered.

Yet Another Way To Create Unique Indexes On PK's

Method 4:   Create Unique Index

```
SQL> ALTER TABLE IOUW
  2         DISABLE CONSTRAINT PK_IOUW;
```

Table altered.

```
SQL> CREATE UNIQUE      INDEX PK_IOUW
  2          ON         IOUW(ID)
  3          TABLESPACE USER_INDEX
  4          STORAGE    (INITIAL 4K   NEXT 4K);
```

Index created.

```
SQL> @are
```
Enter value for owner: **student15**
Enter value for table: **IoUw**

INDEX_NAME	TABLESPACE_NAME	UNIQUENES
PK_IOUW	USER_INDEX	UNIQUE

Speeding Up The Creation Of Indexes Using NOSORT

```
SQL> CREATE INDEX EMP_EMPNO ON EMP(EMPNO) NOSORT;
CREATE INDEX EMP_EMPNO ON EMP(EMPNO) NOSORT
                                     *
ERROR at line 1:
ORA-01409: NOSORT option may not be used; rows are not
           in ascending order
```

If the rows are loaded sorted ascendingly on the indexed
column(s) on a very large table, you can speed up the
creation time for the index dramatically by using the NOSORT
option. One customer stated they went from 19 days to 7 or
8 hours by using "NOSORT" on a table with 175,000,000 rows.
However, they had to write a program to load the data
into the table sorted ascendingly by the column the
index was on.

```
SQL> CREATE INDEX EMP_EMPNO ON EMP(EMPNO);
CREATE INDEX EMP_EMPNO ON EMP(EMPNO)
                              *
ERROR at line 1:
ORA-01547: failed to allocate extent of size 460 in
tablespace 'user_data'
```

Mama told me there'd be days like this, there'd be days
like this, my Mama said.

A Simple Method Of Creating Indexes Using Prompts

```
SQL> CREATE INDEX &IDXNAME ON
                &TABLENAME(&COLNAME);

Enter value for idxname: EMP_HIREDATE
Enter value for tablename: EMP
Enter value for colname: HIREDATE

Index created.
```

This example can be greatly expanded to prompt for the tablespace, storage clause etc.

> *Do you know how to catch a unique bunny ?*
> *Answer: UNIQUE up on him !*
>
> *Know how you catch a TAME bunny ?*
> *Answer: TAME way.*

Creating An Index On More Than One Column

```
SQL> CREATE INDEX IOUW_CNAME_PHONE
  2          ON    IOUW(CNAME, PHONE)
  3          TABLESPACE USER_INDEX
  4          STORAGE(INITIAL 4K  NEXT 4K);
```

Index created.

The first column of this non-unique concatenated index, CNAME, must be referenced in the "WHERE" clause with no functions placed on the column CNAME, for the index to be used in a query regardless of which optimizer you are using. (Rule Or Cost)

To determine which column of a concatenated index is the **LEADING EDGE** or first column, you can use the following query:

```
SQL> get cb134
  1  BREAK  ON  INDEX_NAME  SKIP  2
  2  SELECT INDEX_NAME,
  3         COLUMN_POSITION,
  4         COLUMN_NAME
  5  FROM   SYS.DBA_IND_COLUMNS
  6  WHERE  INDEX_OWNER = UPPER('&Owner') AND
  7         TABLE_NAME  = UPPER('&Table')
  8  ORDER  BY INDEX_NAME, COLUMN_POSITION
  9  /
 10* CLEAR  BREAKS
```

```
SQL> @cb134
Enter value for owner: STUDent15
Enter value for table: ioUW
```

INDEX_NAME	COLUMN_POSITION	COLUMN_NAME
IOUW_CNAME_PHONE	**1**	**CNAME**
	2	PHONE
PK_IOUW	1	ID

Causing Cost-based Optimizer To Make Better Decisions

```
SQL> SELECT *
  2* FROM   IOUW;


ID CNAME            CITY          ST PHONE      RDATE
-- --------------- ------------- -- ---------- ---------
 1 THE BIG O        SAN FRANCISCO CA 4056586500 01-JAN-79
 2 DATABASE CONS.   DALLAS        TX 2143920955 01-JAN-87
 3 MARY SLY BASED   MAUI          HI 4042345678 15-OCT-88
 4 MISS NFORMAL X   OAHU          HI 4041235500 03-MAY-88

SQL> get cb137
  1  SELECT BLEVEL,
  2         LEAF_BLOCKS,
  3         DISTINCT_KEYS,
  4         STATUS
  5  FROM   USER_INDEXES
  6* WHERE  TABLE_NAME = UPPER('&Table')
SQL>/

Enter value for table: iouw

    BLEVEL LEAF_BLOCKS DISTINCT_KEYS STATUS
---------- ----------- ------------- -----------
                                     VALID
                                     VALID

SQL> -- Table or indexes not analyzed as yet

SQL> ANALYZE TABLE IOUW COMPUTE STATISTICS;
Table analyzed.

SQL> @cb137
Enter value for table: iouw
    BLEVEL LEAF_BLOCKS DISTINCT_KEYS STATUS
---------- ----------- ------------- -----------
         0           1             4 VALID
         0           1             4 VALID
```
Notice when you analyze a table, all of the indexes get
analyzed as well.

Determining If Indexes Are Corrupted

```
SQL> UPDATE EMP
  2         SET  JOB = 'CHIEF'
  3         WHERE ROWNUM < 11;

10 rows updated.


SQL> UPDATE EMP
  2         SET JOB = 'INDIAN'
  3         WHERE JOB <> 'CHIEF';

4 rows updated.



SQL> SELECT JOB, COUNT(*)
  2  FROM    EMP
  3  GROUP   BY    JOB;

JOB          COUNT(*)
---------  --------
CHIEF          10
INDIAN          4


SQL> CREATE INDEX INDX_EMP_JOB
  2         ON     EMP(JOB)
  3         TABLESPACE USER_INDEX
  4         STORAGE(INITIAL 2K    NEXT 2K);

Index created.
```

(Continued)

```
SQL> VALIDATE INDEX INDX_EMP_JOB;

Index analyzed.


SQL> DESC INDEX_STATS
 Name                             Null?     Type
 ------------------------------- --------  ----
 HEIGHT                                     NUMBER
 BLOCKS                          NOT NULL  NUMBER
 NAME                            NOT NULL  VARCHAR2(30)
 LF_ROWS                                    NUMBER
 LF_BLKS                                    NUMBER
 LF_ROWS_LEN                                NUMBER
 LF_BLK_LEN                                 NUMBER
 BR_ROWS                                    NUMBER
 BR_BLKS                                    NUMBER
 BR_ROWS_LEN                                NUMBER
 BR_BLK_LEN                                 NUMBER
 DEL_LF_ROWS                                NUMBER
 DEL_LF_ROWS_LEN                            NUMBER
 DISTINCT_KEYS                              NUMBER
 MOST_REPEATED_KEY                          NUMBER
 BTREE_SPACE                                NUMBER
 USED_SPACE                                 NUMBER
 PCT_USED                                   NUMBER
 ROWS_PER_KEY                               NUMBER
 BLKS_GETS_PER_ACCESS                       NUMBER

SQL> SELECT DISTINCT_KEYS,
  2          MOST_REPEATED_KEY,
  3          ROWS_PER_KEY
  4  FROM    INDEX_STATS;

DISTINCT_KEYS MOST_REPEATED_KEY ROWS_PER_KEY
------------- ----------------- ------------
            2                10            7
```

Remember, you now have **10 CHIEFs**, and **4 INDIANs**.
You have two distinct keys(CHIEF and INDIAN), and
CHIEF is the most repeated key occuring ten times.

(Continued)

```
SQL> DESC INDEX_HISTOGRAM
Name                             Null?    Type
-------------------------------- -------- ----
REPEAT_COUNT                              NUMBER
KEYS_WITH_REPEAT_COUNT                    NUMBER



SQL> SELECT *
  2  FROM   INDEX_HISTOGRAM;


REPEAT_COUNT KEYS_WITH_REPEAT_COUNT
------------ ----------------------
           0                      0
           1                      0
           2                      0
           3                      0
           4                      1
           5                      0
           6                      0
           7                      0
           8                      0
           9                      0
          10                      1
          11                      0
          12                      0
          13                      0
          14                      0
          15                      0
16 rows selected.
```

```
You have one index value occurring four times, and
another ten.
```

> *It looks like we have too many CHIEFS, and not enough INDIANS.*

Automatically Populating Number Columns Using Sequences

```
SQL> CREATE SEQUENCE S1
  2           START    WITH   41   NOCACHE;
Sequence created.

SQL> @cb152
SQL> COL     CYCLE_FLAG    FORMAT   A10
SQL> SELECT SUBSTR(SEQUENCE_NAME, 1, 13) "Sequence Name",
  2           MAX_VALUE,
  3           CYCLE_FLAG,
  4           CACHE_SIZE,
  5           LAST_NUMBER
  6  FROM     USER_SEQUENCES
  7  WHERE    SEQUENCE_NAME = UPPER('&Sequence')
  8  /
Enter value for sequence: s1

Sequence Name MAX_VALUE CYCLE_FLAG CACHE_SIZE LAST_NUMBER
------------- --------- ---------- ---------- -----------
S1             1.0E+27 N                   0          41

SQL> INSERT INTO DEPT
  2  VALUES(S1.NEXTVAL, 'IS', 'MAUI');
1 row created.

SQL> SELECT * FROM DEPT WHERE DEPTNO > 30;

 DEPTNO DNAME          LOC
------- -------------- -------------
    40 OPERATIONS     BOSTON
    41 IS             MAUI
SQL> INSERT INTO DEPT
    VALUES(S1.NEXTVAL, 'IS', 'INDY')
SQL> /
1 row created.

SQL> SELECT * FROM DEPT WHERE DEPTNO > 30;

 DEPTNO DNAME          LOC
------- -------------- -------------
    40 OPERATIONS     BOSTON
    41 IS             MAUI
    42 IS             INDY
```

Changing The Value Or Characteristics Of A Sequence

```
SQL> ALTER SEQUENCE S1
  2       MAXVALUE 50
  3       NOCYCLE;
Sequence altered.


SQL> INSERT INTO DEPT
  2   VALUES(S1.NEXTVAL, 'MIS', '&LOC');
Enter value for loc: HANA
1 row created.


SQL> /
Enter value for loc: KIHEI
1 row created.


SQL> /
Enter value for loc: OAHU
1 row created.


SQL> SELECT S1.CURRVAL
  2   FROM    DUAL;

CURRVAL
-------
     49


SQL> get cb156
  1  INSERT INTO DEPT
  2* VALUES(S1.NEXTVAL, 'MIS', '&LOC')
SQL> /
Enter value for loc: KAUAI
1 row created.


SQL> /
Enter value for loc: PAST 50
VALUES(S1.NEXTVAL, 'MIS', 'PAST 50')
       *
ERROR at line 2:
ORA-08004: sequence S1.NEXTVAL exceeds MAXVALUE and cannot
be instantiated
```

(Continued)

```
SQL> /
Enter value for loc: PAST 50
VALUES(S1.NEXTVAL, 'MIS', 'PAST 50')
        *
ERROR at line 2:
ORA-08004: sequence S1.NEXTVAL exceeds MAXVALUE and cannot
be instantiated


SQL> ALTER SEQUENCE S1
  2         NOMAXVALUE
  3         CYCLE;
ALTER SEQUENCE S1
*
ERROR at line 1:
ORA-04015: ascending sequences that CYCLE must specify
MAXVALUE


SQL> ALTER SEQUENCE S1
  2         NOMAXVALUE;

Sequence altered.

SQL> @cb152
SQL> COL    CYCLE_FLAG    FORMAT   A10
SQL> SELECT SUBSTR(SEQUENCE_NAME, 1, 13) "Sequence Name",
  2         MAX_VALUE,
  3         CYCLE_FLAG,
  4         CACHE_SIZE,
  5         LAST_NUMBER
  6  FROM   USER_SEQUENCES
  7  WHERE  SEQUENCE_NAME = UPPER('&Sequence')
  8  /
Enter value for sequence: s1

Sequence Name MAX_VALUE CYCLE_FLAG CACHE_SIZE LAST_NUMBER
------------- --------- ---------- ---------- -----------
S1             1.0E+27 N                   0          51
```

An Alternative To Sequences ("Pistol Pete" Forms Trigger)

Given a table name SEQ_NUMBERS with two columns,
TABLE_NAME, and LAST_NUM with the following data:

SEQ_NUMBERS

TABLE_NAME	LAST_NUM
EMP	9999
DEPT	40

Assume the users want Oracle to automatically plug the
primary key columns with the next number stored in the
SEQ_NUMBERS table in the LAST_NUM column for many tables
in your system. You can write the following trigger
in SQL*Forms V3.0 or Oracle Forms 4.0, 4.5:

```
PRE-INSERT AT THE BLOCK LEVEL
SELECT   LAST_NUM
INTO     :EMP.EMPNO
FROM     SEQ_NUMBERS
WHERE    TABLE_NAME = 'EMP'
FOR      UPDATE;                 -- Lock Row
UPDATE   SEQ_NUMBERS             -- Increment By 1 For Next Emp
         SET LAST_NUM = LAST_NUM + 1
         WHERE TABLE_NAME = 'EMP';
```

This method is OK. However, on a busy system, you
experience "CONTENTION" when two or more users are
attempting to insert rows at the same time and hit the
commit key.

> *During the summer of 1957, I had the real pleasure
> of playing basketball with "The Pistol Pete" at a
> basketball camp in North Carolina, where his father,
> Press, coached many of us. I was "Big Pete" (8th grade),
> and I tried to guard "Little Pete-The-Pistol"
> (4th Grader). It was many years later, 1963 or 1964,
> while serving in the United States Navy, I saw
> Pete's picture on the cover of Sports Illustrated,
> and I learned he played basketball at **LSU**.*
> *Hence, **L**ock-**S**elect-**U**pdate.*

Creating A Snapshot

```
SQL> CONNECT STUDENT1/STUDENT1

Connected.

SQL> SELECT * FROM DEPT ORDER BY DEPTNO;

 DEPTNO DNAME          LOC
 ------ -------------- -------------
     10 ACCOUNTING     NEW YORK
     20 RESEARCH       DALLAS
     30 SALES          CHICAGO
     40 OPERATIONS     BOSTON
     99 MIS            STUDENT1

SQL> CONNECT STUDENT15/STUDENT15

Connected.

SQL> get cb162
  1   CREATE SNAPSHOT LOG ON STUDENT1.DEPT /* NOT REMOTE */
  2          TABLESPACE   USER_DATA
  3*         STORAGE(INITIAL 4K   NEXT 4K)
SQL> /

Snapshot log created.

SQL> CREATE SNAPSHOT DEPT_LIKE_STUDENT1
  2          TABLESPACE   USER_DATA
  3          STORAGE(INITIAL 4K   NEXT 4K)
  4          USING INDEX
  5          TABLESPACE USER_INDEX
  6          STORAGE(INITIAL 4K   NEXT 4K)
  7          REFRESH FAST
  8          START WITH SYSDATE
  9          NEXT SYSDATE + 1/96   /*  EVERY 15 MINUTES   */
 10   AS     SELECT *
 11          FROM   STUDENT1.DEPT;

Snapshot created.
```

(Continued)

```
Following objects created automatically by CREATE SNAPSHOT.
SQL> get cb165
    1  COL     OBJECT_NAME      FORMAT A27
    2  BREAK   ON               OBJECT_TYPE   SKIP  1
    3  SELECT OBJECT_TYPE,
    4         OBJECT_NAME
    5  FROM   USER_OBJECTS
    6  WHERE  OBJECT_NAME      LIKE '%DEPT_LIKE%'
    7  ORDER  BY OBJECT_TYPE, OBJECT_NAME
    8  /
    9* CLEAR  BREAKS
SQL> @cb165
OBJECT_TYPE     OBJECT_NAME
--------------- ---------------------------

INDEX           I_SNAP$_DEPT_LIKE_STUDENT1

TABLE           SNAP$_DEPT_LIKE_STUDENT1

VIEW            DEPT_LIKE_STUDENT1
                MVIEW$_DEPT_LIKE_STUDENT1


SQL> SELECT OBJECT_NAME, OBJECT_TYPE
    2  FROM   SYS.DBA_OBJECTS
    3  WHERE  OBJECT_NAME LIKE 'TLOG$%';
OBJECT_NAME                      OBJECT_TYPE
--------------------------       ------------

TLOG$_DEPT                       TRIGGER


INDEX:
SQL> get cb167
    1  COL     INDEX_NAME          FORMAT    A26
    2  COL     TABLE_NAME          FORMAT    A24
    3  SELECT INDEX_NAME,
    4         TABLE_NAME,
    5         UNIQUENESS
    6  FROM   USER_INDEXES
    7* WHERE  INDEX_NAME LIKE '%SNAP$%'
SQL> @cb167
INDEX_NAME                       TABLE_NAME                 UNIQUENES
--------------------------       ------------------------   --------

I_SNAP$_DEPT_LIKE_STUDENT1 SNAP$_DEPT_LIKE_STUDENT1 UNIQUE
```

(Continued)

```
TABLE:
SQL> SELECT * FROM SNAP$_DEPT_LIKE_STUDENT1;

 DEPTNO DNAME          LOC            M_ROW$$
 ------- -------------- -------------- --------------------
     10 ACCOUNTING     NEW YORK       00000287.0000.0006
     20 RESEARCH       DALLAS         00000287.0001.0006
     30 SALES          CHICAGO        00000287.0002.0006
     40 OPERATIONS     BOSTON         00000287.0003.0006
     99 MIS            STUDENT1       00000287.000E.0006
```

Just for grins, let's take a closer look at the actual
ROWID's in STUDENT1's DEPT table and see if they are
the same as the ROWIDs in SNAP$_DEPT_LIKE_STUDENT1.

```
SQL> SELECT DEPTNO, DNAME, LOC, ROWID
  2  FROM    STUDENT1.DEPT;

 DEPTNO DNAME          LOC            ROWID
 ------- -------------- -------------- --------------------
     10 ACCOUNTING     NEW YORK       00000287.0000.0006
     20 RESEARCH       DALLAS         00000287.0001.0006
     30 SALES          CHICAGO        00000287.0002.0006
     40 OPERATIONS     BOSTON         00000287.0003.0006
     99 MIS            STUDENT1       00000287.000E.0006
```

```
VIEWS:
SQL> SET HEADING OFF
SQL> get cb169
  1  SELECT *
  2  FROM    USER_VIEWS
  3  WHERE   VIEW_NAME LIKE 'DEPT_LIKE%' OR
  4*         VIEW_NAME LIKE '%MVIEW$%'
SQL> /

DEPT_LIKE_STUDENT1                        88
select "DEPTNO","DNAME","LOC" from
"STUDENT15"."SNAP$_DEPT_LIKE_STUDENT1" with r

MVIEW$_DEPT_LIKE_STUDENT1                 67
select "DEPTNO","DNAME","LOC", rowid m_row$$ FROM
STUDENT1.DEPT
```

(Continued)

```
TRIGGER:

SQL> get cb172
  1  SELECT OWNER,
  2         TRIGGER_TYPE,
  3         TRIGGERING_EVENT,
  4         TABLE_NAME
  5  FROM   SYS.DBA_TRIGGERS
  6* WHERE  TRIGGER_NAME = 'TLOG$_DEPT'
SQL> /
```

```
                                                 TABLE
OWNER     TRIGGER_TYPE    TRIGGERING_EVENT       _NAME
--------  --------------  ----------------------  -----
STUDENT1  AFTER EACH ROW  INSERT OR UPDATE OR DELETE  DEPT
```

```
SQL> SET LONG 300
SQL> SELECT TRIGGER_BODY
  2  FROM   SYS.DBA_TRIGGERS
  3* WHERE  TRIGGER_NAME = 'TLOG$_DEPT';
```

```
TRIGGER_BODY
-----------------------------------------------------------------
declare    dmltype char;   begin     if      inserting then
dmltype := 'I';     elsi
f  updating  then  dmltype := 'U';     elsif  deleting  then
dmltype := 'D';      en
d if;    insert into "STUDENT1"."MLOG$_DEPT" (m_row$$,
dmltype$$)      values (:
old.rowid, dmltype);  end;
```

> *After receiving a pair of $1,500 anteater cowboy boots, Roy walked into the kitchen and sat down for dinner. Dale told Roy to leave his boots on the porch since they were muddy. A hungry mountain lion grabbed the boots and ran. Next AM, Dale exclaims as Roy is on Trigger with the dead lion, "Pardon me Roy, is that the cat that chewed your new shoes?"*

Forcing A Snapshot To Be Refreshed

```
16:20:38 SQL> SELECT * FROM SNAP$_DEPT_LIKE_STUDENT1;
 DEPTNO DNAME          LOC           M_ROW$$
------- -------------- ------------- -------------------
     10 ACCOUNTING     NEW YORK      00000287.0000.0006
     20 RESEARCH       DALLAS        00000287.0001.0006
     30 SALES          CHICAGO       00000287.0002.0006
     40 OPERATIONS     BOSTON        00000287.0003.0006
     99 MIS            STUDENT1      00000287.000E.0006
16:20:58 SQL> CONNECT STUDENT1/STUDENT1
Connected.
16:22:27 SQL> INSERT INTO DEPT VALUES(55,'IS','DAYTONA');
1 row created.

16:23:04 SQL> CONNECT STUDENT15/STUDENT15
Connected.
16:23:19 SQL> SELECT * FROM DEPT_LIKE_STUDENT1;
 DEPTNO DNAME          LOC
------- -------------- -------------
     10 ACCOUNTING     NEW YORK
     20 RESEARCH       DALLAS
     30 SALES          CHICAGO
     40 OPERATIONS     BOSTON
     99 MIS            STUDENT1
```

Notice that **"DAYTONA"** does not show up in your snapshot since it refreshes every 15 minutes. Well, I don't have 15 minutes ! Lord, please grant be patience NOW !! So, force your snapshot to refresh 6 minutes after the insert.

```
16:28:33 SQL> EXECUTE
DBMS_SNAPSHOT.REFRESH('DEPT_LIKE_STUDENT1','C')
PL/SQL procedure successfully completed.
16:29:31 SQL> SELECT * FROM DEPT_LIKE_STUDENT1;
 DEPTNO DNAME          LOC
------- -------------- -------------
     10 ACCOUNTING     NEW YORK
     20 RESEARCH       DALLAS
     30 SALES          CHICAGO
     40 OPERATIONS     BOSTON
     55 IS             DAYTONA
     99 MIS            STUDENT1
6 rows selected.
```

Creating Test Tables

```
SQL> CREATE TABLE EMP_LIKE AS  /* LOOKS JUST LIKE EMP */
          SELECT *
          FROM   EMP;
```
Table created.

```
SQL> CREATE TABLE EMP_LIKE2 AS  /* LIKE EMP WITH 4 ROWS */
          SELECT *
          FROM   EMP
          WHERE ROWNUM < 5;
```
Table created.

```
SQL> CREATE TABLE EMP_LIKE3 AS  /* EMPNO'S MULTIPLE OF 3 */
          SELECT *
          FROM   EMP
          WHERE MOD(EMPNO,3) = 0;
```
Table created.

```
SQL> SELECT EMPNO, ENAME
  2  FROM   EMP_LIKE3;
```

EMPNO	ENAME	
7902	MARTIN	7+9+0+2=18 And 18/3=6 **R=0**
7902	BLAKE	
7902	CLARK	
7902	SCOTT	
7839	KING	7+8+3+9=27 And 27/3=9 **R=0**
7902	FORD	

6 rows selected.

```
SQL> CREATE TABLE EMP_LIKE4 AS  /*  NO ROWS              */
          SELECT *
          FROM    EMP            /*  ONE NEVER EQUALS TWO  */
          WHERE  1 = 2;
```
Table created.

Creating Tables

```
SQL> get cb173
  1   CREATE TABLE SPRINT_CARS
  2        (SNUM              NUMBER(2,0),
  3         SNAME             VARCHAR2(20) DEFAULT 'OUTLAW',
  4         ENGINE_SIZE       NUMBER(3,0)  DEFAULT 360,
  5         HORSE_POWER       NUMBER(3)    DEFAULT 600,
  6         MAX_SPEED         NUMBER(6,3),
  7         WING              CHAR(1)      DEFAULT 'N',
  8         CONSTRAINT        PK_SPRINT_CARS_CAR_SNUM
  9                           PRIMARY KEY(SNUM)
 10                           USING       INDEX
 11                           TABLESPACE  USER_INDEX
 12                           STORAGE     (INITIAL 4K
 13                                        NEXT    4K),
 14         CONSTRAINT        CK_SPRINT_CARS_WING
 15                           CHECK(WING IN('Y','N')))
 16   TABLESPACE             USER_DATA
 17   STORAGE                (INITIAL 4K   NEXT 4K)
 18   PARALLEL               (DEGREE 4)
 19*  CACHE
SQL> /
```

Table created.

```
SQL> SELECT  TABLESPACE_NAME,
  2          DEGREE,
  3          CACHE,
  4          PCT_FREE
  5  FROM    USER_TABLES
  6  WHERE   TABLE_NAME = UPPER('&Table');
```
Enter value for table: **SPRINT_CARS**

TABLESPACE_NAME	DEGREE	CACHE	PCT_FREE
USER_DATA	4	Y	10

(Continued)

The primary key constraint clause in the create table
statement, causes Oracle to create a unique index with
the same name as the name of the constraint. And, if you
don't name your constraints, Oracle names them for
you. (SYS_C9999) The nines represent any number from
0 through 9.

```
SQL> get are
  1   SELECT INDEX_NAME,
  2          TABLESPACE_NAME,
  3          UNIQUENESS
  4   FROM   SYS.DBA_INDEXES
  5   WHERE  OWNER = UPPER('&Owner') AND
  6*         TABLE_NAME = UPPER('&Table')
SQL> /
Enter value for owner: student15
Enter value for table: sprint_CARS

INDEX_NAME                      TABLESPACE_NAME UNIQUENES
------------------------------- --------------- ---------
PK_SPRINT_CARS_CAR_SNUM         USER_INDEX      UNIQUE


SQL> get cons
  1   SET     VERIFY     OFF
  2   COL     CONSTRAINT_NAME        FORMAT    A23
  3   COL     CONSTRAINT_TYPE        HEADING TYPE    FORMAT A4
  4   COL     SEARCH_CONDITION       FORMAT    A25
  5   SELECT CONSTRAINT_NAME,
  6          CONSTRAINT_TYPE,
  7          SEARCH_CONDITION
  8   FROM   USER_CONSTRAINTS
  9*  WHERE  TABLE_NAME = UPPER('&Table')
SQL> @cons
Enter value for table: SpRINT_cars

CONSTRAINT_NAME          TYPE SEARCH_CONDITION
------------------------ ---- -------------------------
PK_SPRINT_CARS_CAR_SNUM  P
CK_SPRINT_CARS_WING      C    WING IN('Y','N')
```

(Continued)

The default clause in the create table statement produces
the following:

```
SQL> get cb175
  1  COL     COLUMN_NAME    FORMAT   A15
  2  COL     DATA_DEFAULT   FORMAT   A25
  3  SELECT COLUMN_NAME,
  4         DATA_DEFAULT
  5  FROM    USER_TAB_COLUMNS
  6* WHERE   TABLE_NAME = UPPER('&Table')
SQL> @cb175
Enter value for table: sprint_cars

COLUMN_NAME      DATA_DEFAULT
---------------  -------------------------
SNUM
SNAME            'OUTLAW'
ENGINE_SIZE      360
HORSE_POWER      600
MAX_SPEED
WING             'N'
6 rows selected.

SQL> INSERT INTO SPRINT_CARS
          (SNUM,ENGINE_SIZE,WING,MAX_SPEED)
      VALUES(1,485,'Y',195);
1 row created.
SQL> COL WING FORMAT A4

SQL> SELECT *
  2  FROM    SPRINT_CARS;

SNUM SNAME   ENGINE_SIZE HORSE_POWER MAX_SPEED WING
---- ------  ----------- ----------- --------- ----
   1 OUTLAW          485         600       195 Y
```

Adding Columns To A Table

```
SQL> DESC SPRINT_CARS
 Name                                    Null?    Type
 ------------------------------------ -------- ----
 SNUM                                    NOT NULL NUMBER(2)
 SNAME                                            VARCHAR2(20)
 ENGINE_SIZE                                      NUMBER(3)
 HORSE_POWER                                      NUMBER(3)
 MAX_SPEED                                        NUMBER(6,3)
 WING                                             CHAR(1)
```

```
SQL> ALTER TABLE SPRINT_CARS ADD FUEL_TYPE CHAR(1);
```

```
Table altered.
```

```
SQL> DESC SPRINT_CARS
 Name                                    Null?    Type
 ------------------------------------ -------- ----
 SNUM                                    NOT NULL NUMBER(2)
 SNAME                                            VARCHAR2(20)
 ENGINE_SIZE                                      NUMBER(3)
 HORSE_POWER                                      NUMBER(3)
 MAX_SPEED                                        NUMBER(6,3)
 WING                                             CHAR(1)
 FUEL_TYPE                                        CHAR(1)
```

Changing Datatypes Of Columns

```
SQL> DESC SPRINT_CARS
 Name                                    Null?    Type
 ------------------------------- -------- ----
 SNUM                                    NOT NULL NUMBER(2)
 SNAME                                            VARCHAR2(20)
 ENGINE_SIZE                                      NUMBER(3)
 HORSE_POWER                                      NUMBER(3)
 MAX_SPEED                                        NUMBER(6,3)
 WING                                             CHAR(1)
 FUEL_TYPE                                        CHAR(1)

SQL> ALTER TABLE SPRINT_CARS MODIFY ENGINE_SIZE VARCHAR2(3);
ALTER TABLE SPRINT_CARS MODIFY ENGINE_SIZE VARCHAR2(3)
                               *
ERROR at line 1:
ORA-01439: column to be modified must be empty to change
datatype

SQL> UPDATE SPRINT_CARS  /*  Think Carefully Here !@#!  */
  2       SET ENGINE_SIZE = NULL;
1 row updated.


SQL> ALTER TABLE SPRINT_CARS MODIFY ENGINE_SIZE VARCHAR2(3);

Table altered.


SQL> DESC SPRINT_CARS
 Name                                    Null?    Type
 ------------------------------- -------- ----
 SNUM                                    NOT NULL NUMBER(2)
 SNAME                                            VARCHAR2(20)
 ENGINE_SIZE                                      VARCHAR2(3)
 HORSE_POWER                                      NUMBER(3)
 MAX_SPEED                                        NUMBER(6,3)
 WING                                             CHAR(1)
 FUEL_TYPE                                        CHAR(1)
```

Lengthening Columns

```
SQL> DESC SPRINT_CARS
 Name                              Null?    Type
 -------------------------------- -------- ----
 SNUM                             NOT NULL NUMBER(2)
 SNAME                                     VARCHAR2(20)
 ENGINE_SIZE                               VARCHAR2(3)
 HORSE_POWER                               NUMBER(3)
 MAX_SPEED                                 NUMBER(6,3)
 WING                                      CHAR(1)
 FUEL_TYPE                                 CHAR(1)
```

```
SQL> ALTER TABLE SPRINT_CARS MODIFY SNAME VARCHAR2(25);
```

```
Table altered.
```

```
SQL> DESC SPRINT_CARS
 Name                              Null?    Type
 -------------------------------- -------- ----
 SNUM                             NOT NULL NUMBER(2)
 SNAME                                     VARCHAR2(25)
 ENGINE_SIZE                               VARCHAR2(3)
 HORSE_POWER                               NUMBER(3)
 MAX_SPEED                                 NUMBER(6,3)
 WING                                      CHAR(1)
 FUEL_TYPE                                 CHAR(1)
```

Enforcing Business Rules Using Check Constraints

```
SQL> ALTER TABLE SPRINT_CARS
  2         ADD    CONSTRAINT  CK_SPRINT_CARS_HORSE_POWER
  3*         CHECK(HORSE_POWER BETWEEN 100 AND 980);

Table altered.


SQL> get cons
  1   SET    VERIFY    OFF
  2   COL    CONSTRAINT_NAME      FORMAT    A26
  3   COL    CONSTRAINT_TYPE      HEADING TYPE   FORMAT A4
  4   COL    SEARCH_CONDITION     FORMAT    A31
  5   SELECT CONSTRAINT_NAME,
  6          CONSTRAINT_TYPE,
  7          SEARCH_CONDITION
  8   FROM   USER_CONSTRAINTS
  9*  WHERE  TABLE_NAME = UPPER('&Table')
SQL> @cons
Enter value for table: sprint_cars

CONSTRAINT_NAME                TYPE SEARCH_CONDITION
-------------------------- ---- ---------------------------
PK_SPRINT_CARS_CAR_SNUM    P
CK_SPRINT_CARS_WING        C WING IN('Y','N')
CK_SPRINT_CARS_HORSE_POWER C HORSE_POWER BETWEEN 100 AND 980


SQL> UPDATE SPRINT_CARS      /*  OK, I Have Some Missouri */
  2  SET HORSE_POWER = 995   /*  Blood In Me              */
  3  WHERE SNUM      = 1;
UPDATE SPRINT_CARS
*
ERROR at line 1:
ORA-02290: check constraint
(STUDENT15.CK_SPRINT_CARS_HORSE_POWER) violated
```

Dropping Constraints

```
SQL> GET cons
  1  SET     VERIFY     OFF
  2  COL     CONSTRAINT_NAME      FORMAT    A26
  3  COL     CONSTRAINT_TYPE      HEADING TYPE   FORMAT A4
  4  COL     SEARCH_CONDITION     FORMAT    A31
  5  SELECT  CONSTRAINT_NAME,
  6          CONSTRAINT_TYPE,
  7          SEARCH_CONDITION,
  8          STATUS
  9  FROM    USER_CONSTRAINTS
 10* WHERE   TABLE_NAME = UPPER('&Table')
SQL> @cons
```

Enter value for table: **sprint_cars**

CONSTRAINT_NAME	TYPE	SEARCH_CONDITION	STATUS
PK_SPRINT_CARS_CAR_SNUM	P		ENABLED
CK_SPRINT_CARS_WING	C	WING IN('Y','N')	ENABLED
CK_SPRINT_CARS_HORSE_POWER	C	HORSE_POWER BETWEEN 100 AND 980	ENABLED

```
SQL> ALTER TABLE SPRINT_CARS
  2       DROP  CONSTRAINT CK_SPRINT_CARS_HORSE_POWER;
Table altered.

SQL> @cons
```
Enter value for table: **sprint_CArS**

CONSTRAINT_NAME	TYPE	SEARCH_CONDITION	STATUS
PK_SPRINT_CARS_CAR_SNUM	P		ENABLED
CK_SPRINT_CARS_WING	C	WING IN('Y','N')	ENABLED

> *Which way did he go? Which way did he go?*
> *I say, I say, I think he went that away.*

Disabling PK Constraints

```
SQL> ALTER TABLE    SPRINT_CARS
          DISABLE PRIMARY KEY;
```
Table altered.

- OR -

```
SQL> ALTER TABLE SPRINT_CARS
  2          DISABLE CONSTRAINT
  3          PK_SPRINT_CARS_CAR_SNUM;
```
Table altered.

You accomplish two things here. You disable the primary key
constraint, and the primary key unique index gets dropped
as well. Naturally, then, when you enable the primary key
constraint, the primary key unique index is created
again. This can be very time consuming on large tables.

```
SQL> @cons
```
Enter value for table: **sprint_cars**

CONSTRAINT_NAME	TYPE	SEARCH_CONDITION	STATUS
PK_SPRINT_CARS_CAR_SNUM	P		**DISABLED**
CK_SPRINT_CARS_WING	C	WING IN('Y','N')	ENABLED

```
SQL> get are
  1  SELECT INDEX_NAME,
  2         TABLESPACE_NAME,
  3         UNIQUENESS
  4  FROM   SYS.DBA_INDEXES
  5  WHERE  OWNER = UPPER('&Owner') AND
  6*        TABLE_NAME = UPPER('&Table')
SQL> @are
```
Enter value for owner: **student15**
Enter value for table: **sprint_cars**

no rows selected

THE PRIMARY KEY UNIQUE INDEX GETS DROPPED WHEN THE
PRIMARY KEY CONSTRAINT GETS DISABLED.

Enabling PK Constraints

```
SQL> ALTER TABLE SPRINT_CARS
  2         ENABLE PRIMARY KEY;
```

Table altered.

- OR -

```
SQL> ALTER TABLE SPRINT_CARS
  2         ENABLE CONSTRAINT
  3         PK_SPRINT_CARS_CAR_SNUM;
```

Table altered.

```
SQL> @cons
```
Enter value for table: **sprint_cars**

CONSTRAINT_NAME	TYPE	SEARCH_CONDITION	STATUS
PK_SPRINT_CARS_CAR_SNUM	P		**ENABLED**
CK_SPRINT_CARS_WING	C	WING IN('Y','N')	ENABLED

```
SQL> get are
  1   SELECT INDEX_NAME,
  2          TABLESPACE_NAME,
  3          UNIQUENESS
  4   FROM   SYS.DBA_INDEXES
  5   WHERE  OWNER = UPPER('&Owner') AND
  6*         TABLE_NAME = UPPER('&Table')
SQL> /
```
Enter value for owner: **student15**
Enter value for table: **sprint_cars**

INDEX_NAME	TABLESPACE_NAME	UNIQUENES
PK_SPRINT_CARS_CAR_SNUM	USER_DATA	UNIQUE

Adding Column Defaults

```
SQL> SELECT COLUMN_NAME,
  2         DATA_DEFAULT
  3  FROM   USER_TAB_COLUMNS
  4  WHERE  TABLE_NAME = UPPER('&Table');
Enter value for table: SPRINT_CARS

COLUMN_NAME     DATA_DEFAULT
--------------- ------------------------
SNUM
SNAME           'OUTLAW'
ENGINE_SIZE     360
HORSE_POWER     600
MAX_SPEED
WING            'N'
FUEL_TYPE
7 rows selected.

SQL> ALTER TABLE SPRINT_CARS
  2         MODIFY FUEL_TYPE
  3*        DEFAULT 'M';
    DEFAULT 'M'
              *
ERROR at line 3:
ORA-01401: inserted value too large for column

SQL> DESC SPRINT_CARS
 Name                                      Null?    Type
 ----------------------------------------- -------- ----
 SNUM                                      NOT NULL NUMBER(2)
 .......                                   ........ ........
 FUEL_TYPE                                          CHAR(1)

SQL> ALTER TABLE SPRINT_CARS     /* Must Be CHAR(2)   */
  2         MODIFY FUEL_TYPE     /* Or VARCHAR2(2)     */
  3         VARCHAR2(2);
Table altered.

SQL> ALTER TABLE SPRINT_CARS
  2         MODIFY FUEL_TYPE
  3         DEFAULT 'M';
Table altered.
```

Deleting Column Defaults

```
SQL> get def
  1  SELECT COLUMN_NAME,
  2         DATA_DEFAULT
  3  FROM   USER_TAB_COLUMNS
  4* WHERE  TABLE_NAME = UPPER('&Table')
SQL> /
Enter value for table: sprint_cars

COLUMN_NAME       DATA_DEFAULT
---------------   ------------------------
SNUM
SNAME             'OUTLAW'
ENGINE_SIZE       360
HORSE_POWER       600
MAX_SPEED
WING              'N'
FUEL_TYPE         'M'
7 rows selected.

SQL> ALTER TABLE SPRINT_CARS
  2         MODIFY FUEL_TYPE
  3         DEFAULT NULL;
Table altered.
SQL> get def
  1  SELECT COLUMN_NAME,
  2         DATA_DEFAULT
  3  FROM   USER_TAB_COLUMNS
  4* WHERE  TABLE_NAME = UPPER('&Table')
SQL> /
Enter value for table: sprint_CARS

COLUMN_NAME       DATA_DEFAULT
---------------   ------------------------
SNUM
SNAME             'OUTLAW'
ENGINE_SIZE       360
HORSE_POWER       600
MAX_SPEED
WING              'N'
FUEL_TYPE
7 rows selected.
```

A Common Problem Encountered While Trying To Alter

SQL> GRANT ALL ON SPRINT_CARS TO STUDENT1;

Grant succeeded.

Assume STUDENT1 logs into SQL*Plus and issues the following command:

> sqlplus student1/student1

SQL> UPDATE STUDENT15.SPRINT_CARS
               SET FUEL_TYPE = 'X';

1 row updated.

STUDENT1 now has all rows in the STUDENT15.SPRINT_CARS table locked. Watch what happens, when STUDENT15 attempts to ALTER his/her table.

SQL> ALTER TABLE SPRINT_CARS
   2   ADD COST_TO_BUILD NUMBER(10,2);
ALTER TABLE SPRINT_CARS
*
ERROR at line 1:
ORA-00054: resource busy and acquire with NOWAIT specified

Hopefully, it is very apparent that active production tables should be ALTERED only at non-peak times.

> *One time I interviewed for a programmer analyst position in a candle factory, but was very disappointed when I learned I would have to work WICK ENDS.*

Changing The Name Of A Constraint

```
SQL> ALTER TABLE SPRINT_CARS
  2         MODIFY MAX_SPEED NOT NULL;
       MODIFY MAX_SPEED NOT NULL
                    *
ERROR at line 2:
ORA-01449: column contains NULL values; cannot alter to NOT
NULL
SQL> UPDATE SPRINT_CARS  /* Be Careful, All Rows Updated */
  2   SET MAX_SPEED = 195;
1 row updated.

SQL> ALTER TABLE SPRINT_CARS
  2         MODIFY MAX_SPEED NOT NULL;
Table altered.
```

Remember, if you do not name your constraint, Oracle names it for you. i.e. **SYS_C006906** is the name of your NOT NULL constraint on the MAX_SPEED column.

```
SQL> @cons
Enter value for table: sprint_cars
```

CONSTRAINT_NAME	TYPE	SEARCH_CONDITION	STATUS
PK_SPRINT_CARS_CAR_SNUM	P		ENABLED
CK_SPRINT_CARS_WING	C	WING IN('Y','N')	ENABLED
SYS_C006906	**C**	**MAX_SPEED IS NOT NULL**	**ENABLED**

```
SQL> ALTER TABLE SPRINT_CARS
  2         MODIFY MAX_SPEED
  3         CONSTRAINT NN_SPRINT_CARS_MS
  4*        NOT NULL;
Table altered.

SQL> @cons
Enter value for table: sprint_cars
```

CONSTRAINT_NAME	TYPE	SEARCH_CONDITION	STATUS
PK_SPRINT_CARS_CAR_SNUM	P		ENABLED
CK_SPRINT_CARS_WING	C	WING IN('Y','N')	ENABLED
NN_SPRINT_CARS_MS	**C**	**MAX_SPEED IS NOT NULL**	**ENABLED**

Creating Views

```
SQL> CREATE VIEW R2D2 AS
  2          SELECT EMPNO, ENAME, DEPTNO
  3          FROM    EMP;
View created.

SQL> DESC R2D2
 Name                                          Null?     Type
 ------------------------------------- -------- ----
 EMPNO                                         NOT NULL NUMBER(4)
 ENAME                                                  VARCHAR2(10)
 DEPTNO                                                 NUMBER(2)

SQL> SET LONG 45
SQL> SELECT *
  2  FROM    USER_VIEWS
  3* WHERE   VIEW_NAME = 'R2D2';

VIEW_NAME   TEXT_LENGTH TEXT
---------   ------------ -------------------------------------
R2D2                  46 SELECT EMPNO, ENAME, DEPTNO
                         FROM    EMP
SQL> SELECT *  FROM R2D2 WHERE ROWNUM < 3;

  EMPNO ENAME         DEPTNO
 ------- ---------- -------
   7369 SMITH            20
   7499 ALLEN            30

SQL> UPDATE R2D2
  2  SET     ENAME = 'HADACALL'
  3  WHERE   ROWNUM < 3;
2 rows updated.

SQL> SELECT * FROM R2D2 WHERE ROWNUM < 3;

  EMPNO ENAME         DEPTNO
 ------- ---------- -------
   7369 HADACALL         20
   7499 HADACALL         30
```

Creating Views Using Personalized Column Names

```
SQL> CREATE VIEW R2D3(ENO, NAME, SALARY, TITLE, DOH)
  2  AS
  3  SELECT EMPNO, ENAME, SAL, JOB, HIREDATE
  4  FROM    EMP;

View created.

SQL> SELECT *
  2  FROM    R2D3
  3  WHERE   ROWNUM < 5;

    ENO NAME         SALARY TITLE      DOH
------- ---------- ------- ---------  ---------
   7369 SMITH          800 CLERK      17-DEC-80
   7499 ALLEN         1600 SALESMAN   20-FEB-81
   7521 WARD          1250 SALESMAN   22-FEB-81
   7566 JONES         2975 MANAGER    02-APR-81

SQL> CREATE SYNONYM ROCKY FOR R2D3;

Synonym created.

SQL> SELECT *
  2  FROM    ROCKY
  3  WHERE   ROWNUM < 2;
    ENO NAME         SALARY TITLE      DOH
------- ---------- ------- ---------  ---------
   7369 SMITH          800 CLERK      17-DEC-80

SQL> GRANT SELECT ON ROCKY TO STUDENT1;
Grant succeeded.

SQL> CONNECT STUDENT1/STUDENT1
Connected.
SQL> SELECT *
  2  FROM    STUDENT15.ROCKY
  3  WHERE   ROWNUM < 2;

    ENO NAME         SALARY TITLE      DOH
------- ---------- ------- ---------  ---------
   7369 SMITH          800 CLERK      17-DEC-80
```

Preventing Accidental Deletion Of Rows In A View

The whole purpose of the "WITH CHECK OPTION" is to keep someone from accidentally updating rows out of their view.

```
SQL> CREATE VIEW WCO
  2  AS
  3  SELECT  EMPNO, ENAME, SAL, DEPTNO
  4  FROM    EMP
  5  WHERE   DEPTNO = 20
  6* WITH    CHECK OPTION;
View created.

SQL> SELECT *
  2  FROM    WCO;

    EMPNO ENAME           SAL  DEPTNO
   ------- ---------- ------- -------
     7369 SMITH           800      20
     7566 JONES          2975      20
     7788 SCOTT          3000      20
     7876 ADAMS          1100      20
     7902 FORD           3000      20

SQL> UPDATE WCO
  2  SET     SAL = 5500
  3  WHERE   ENAME = 'FORD';
1 row updated.

SQL> SELECT *
  2  FROM    WCO
  3  WHERE   SAL = 5500;

    EMPNO ENAME           SAL  DEPTNO
   ------- ---------- ------- -------
     7902 FORD           5500      20

SQL> UPDATE WCO
  2  SET     DEPTNO = 10;
SET     DEPTNO = 10
                 *

ERROR at line 2:
ORA-01402: view WITH CHECK OPTION where-clause violation
```

Danger Of Omitting The "With Check Option" In A View

```
SQL> CREATE VIEW NO_CHECKY
  2  AS
  3  SELECT EMPNO, ENAME, SAL, DEPTNO
  4  FROM    EMP
  5* WHERE   DEPTNO = 20;
```

View created.

```
SQL> SELECT *
  2  FROM    NO_CHECKY;
```

```
    EMPNO ENAME            SAL  DEPTNO
   ------- ---------- ------- -------
     7369 SMITH            800      20
     7566 JONES           2975      20
     7788 SCOTT           3000      20
     7876 ADAMS           1100      20
     7902 FORD            3000      20
```

```
SQL> UPDATE NO_CHECKY
  2  SET     SAL = 5500
  3  WHERE   ENAME = 'FORD';
```
1 row updated.

```
SQL> SELECT *
  2  FROM    NO_CHECKY
  3  WHERE   SAL = 5500;
```

```
    EMPNO ENAME            SAL  DEPTNO
   ------- ---------- ------- -------
     7902 FORD            5500      20
```

```
SQL> UPDATE NO_CHECKY  /*  Way To Go Dude */
  2  SET     DEPTNO = 10;
```
5 rows updated.

```
SQL> SELECT *
  2  FROM    NO_CHECKY;
```

no rows selected

Creating Views On Multiple Tables

```
SQL> CREATE VIEW EMP_AND_DEPT AS
  2   SELECT ENAME, LOC
  3   FROM     EMP,    DEPT
  4   WHERE   EMP.DEPTNO = DEPT.DEPTNO;
View created.

SQL> DESC EMP_AND_DEPT
 Name                                    Null?    Type
 ------------------------------------ -------- ----
 ENAME                                           VARCHAR2(10)
 LOC                                             VARCHAR2(13)

SQL> SELECT *
  2   FROM     EMP_AND_DEPT;
ENAME        LOC
---------- -------------
SMITH        NEW YORK
JONES        NEW YORK
SCOTT        NEW YORK
ADAMS        NEW YORK
FORD         NEW YORK
KING         NEW YORK
CLARK        NEW YORK
MILLER       NEW YORK
ALLEN        CHICAGO
BLAKE        CHICAGO
MARTIN       CHICAGO
JAMES        CHICAGO
TURNER       CHICAGO
WARD         CHICAGO
14 rows selected.

SQL> UPDATE EMP_AND_DEPT
  2   SET     LOC = 'HANA'
  3   WHERE   ENAME = 'FORD';
UPDATE EMP_AND_DEPT
       *
ERROR at line 1:
ORA-01732: data manipulation operation not legal on this
view
```

Creating Views On Non-Existent Tables

If you ever want to create the views before the tables exist, you can do it with the *"FORCE VIEW"* clause.

```
SQL> CREATE FORCE VIEW EARLY
  2  AS
  3  SELECT CAR_NUM, DRIVER_NUM, DRIVER_NAME
  4  FROM   YOU_GOTTAH_BE_KIDDIN;
```

Warning: View created with compilation errors.

```
SQL> DESC EARLY
```
ERROR:
ORA-04063: view "STUDENT15.EARLY" has errors

```
SQL> SELECT *
  2  FROM   EARLY;
```
FROM   EARLY
*   ***
ERROR at line 2:
ORA-04063: view "STUDENT15.EARLY" has errors

```
SQL> CREATE TABLE YOU_GOTTAH_BE_KIDDIN
  2          (CAR_NUM          NUMBER,
  3           DRIVER_NUM       NUMBER,
  4           DRIVER_NAME      VARCHAR2(25))
  5  TABLESPACE USER_DATA
  6  STORAGE(INITIAL 2K       NEXT 2K);
```
Table created.

```
SQL> INSERT INTO YOU_GOTTAH_BE_KIDDIN
  2          VALUES(44, 1, 'WALT BROWN');
```
1 row created.

```
SQL> SELECT *
  2  FROM   EARLY;
```

CAR_NUM DRIVER_NUM DRIVER_NAME
------- ---------- -------------------------
*   44   1 WALT BROWN*

CHAPTER

6

Last Coffee Break Of The Day Or Constraints PK, FK, Unique, Check, And Not Null

Implementing Constraints

Given the following ERD(Entity Relationship Diagram)
which is LOGICAL:

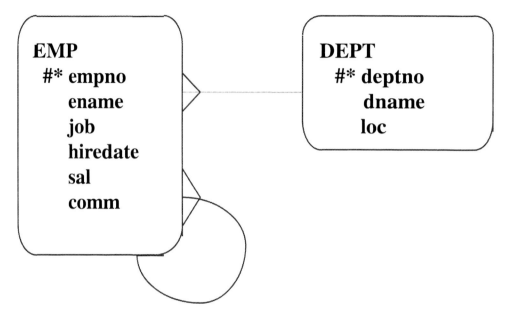

PHYSICAL Table Instance Charts From The Above ERD:

EMP

EMPNO	ENAME	JOB	MGR	HIREDATE	SAL	COMM	DEPTNO
PK			**FK2**				**FK1**
7839	KING	PRES		17-NOV-81	5000		10
7521	WARD	SALESMAN	7698	22-FEB-81	1250	500	30
7698	BLAKE	MANAGER	7839	01-MAY-81	2850		30

DEPT

DEPTNO	DNAME	LOC
PK		
10	ACCOUNTING	NEW YORK
20	RESEARCH	DALLAS

Mickeey to Mineee:
Is that a Mineee
to one ?

Creating Primary Key Constraints

One way of course, is with the CREATE TABLE command which
was discussed in the previous chapter. Another method is to
use the ALTER TABLE command. The following shows how to
create the PRIMARY KEY CONSTRAINTS for both the EMP and DEPT
tables: But first, let's see if any constraints already
exist. SYS_C006908 is a result of the CREATE TABLE command
with a NOT NULL on the empno column.

```
SQL> get cons
    1   SET     VERIFY      OFF
    2   COL     CONSTRAINT_NAME       FORMAT    A26
    3   COL     CONSTRAINT_TYPE       HEADING  TYPE   FORMAT A4
    4   COL     SEARCH_CONDITION      FORMAT    A31
    5   SELECT  CONSTRAINT_NAME,
    6           CONSTRAINT_TYPE,
    7           SEARCH_CONDITION,
    8           STATUS
    9   FROM    USER_CONSTRAINTS
   10*  WHERE   TABLE_NAME = UPPER('&Table')
SQL> @cons
Enter value for table: emp
CONSTRAINT_NAME   TYPE  SEARCH_CONDITION    STATUS
---------------   ----  ----------------    -------

SYS_C006908       C     EMPNO IS NOT NULL  ENABLED
SQL> @cons
Enter value for table: dept
no rows selected
SQL> get cb231
    1   ALTER TABLE EMP
    2          ADD     CONSTRAINT      PK_EMP_EMPNO
    3          PRIMARY KEY(EMPNO)
    4          USING INDEX      /* Index In Separate Tablespace */
    5          TABLESPACE USER_INDEX   /* Very Small Index   */
    6*         STORAGE(INITIAL 2K    NEXT 2K)
SQL> /
Table altered.

SQL> ALTER TABLE DEPT ADD CONSTRAINT PK_DEPT_DEPTNO
    2          PRIMARY KEY(DEPTNO) USING INDEX
    3          TABLESPACE USER_INDEX
    4          STORAGE(INITIAL 2K   NEXT 2K);
Table altered.
```

(Continued)

Oracle creates a unique index on the
primary key column(s) when you CREATE a table using the
primary key constraint,
ALTER a table by adding a primary key constraint, or when
you ALTER a table and ENABLE a primary key constraint.

As a result of adding primary key constraints to both the
EMP and DEPT tables, the following unique indexes are
created for you automatically or *implicitly.*

```
SQL> get are
  1   SELECT INDEX_NAME,
  2          TABLESPACE_NAME,
  3          UNIQUENESS
  4   FROM   SYS.DBA_INDEXES
  5   WHERE  OWNER = UPPER('&Owner') AND
  6*         TABLE_NAME = UPPER('&Table')
SQL> /
Enter value for owner: student15
Enter value for table: emp
```

INDEX_NAME	TABLESPACE_NAME	UNIQUENES
PK_EMP_EMPNO	USER_INDEX	UNIQUE

Notice Oracle names the unique index for the primary key the
same as your constraint name. Refer to the previous page.

```
SQL> @are
Enter value for owner: student15
Enter value for table: dept
```

INDEX_NAME	TABLESPACE_NAME	UNIQUENES
PK_DEPT_DEPTNO	USER_INDEX	UNIQUE

Creating FK Constraints

```
SQL> @cons
Enter value for table: emp
CONSTRAINT_NAME      TYPE     SEARCH_CONDITION      STATUS
---------------      ----     ----------------      ------
SYS_C006908          C        EMPNO IS NOT NULL     ENABLED
PK_EMP_EMPNO         P                              ENABLED

SQL> @cons
Enter value for table: dept
CONSTRAINT_NAME      TYPE     SEARCH_CONDITION      STATUS
---------------      ----     ----------------      -------
PK_DEPT_DEPTNO       P                              ENABLED

SQL> ALTER TABLE      EMP
  2         ADD        CONSTRAINT   FK1_EMP_DEPTNO
  3         FOREIGN    KEY(DEPTNO)
  4         REFERENCES DEPT(DEPTNO);
Table altered.

SQL> ALTER TABLE      EMP
  2         ADD        CONSTRAINT   FK2_EMP_MGR
  3         FOREIGN    KEY(MGR)
  4         REFERENCES EMP(EMPNO);
Table altered.

SQL> @cons
Enter value for table: emp
CONSTRAINT_NAME      TYPE     SEARCH_CONDITION      STATUS
---------------      ----     ----------------      -------
SYS_C006908          C        EMPNO IS NOT NULL     ENABLED
PK_EMP_EMPNO         P                              ENABLED
FK1_EMP_DEPTNO       R                              ENABLED
FK2_EMP_MGR          R                              ENABLED

SQL> ALTER TABLE EMP DISABLE CONSTRAINT FK2_EMP_MGR;
Table altered.

SQL> ALTER TABLE EMP ENABLE CONSTRAINT FK2_EMP_MGR;
Table altered.

SQL> ALTER TABLE EMP DROP CONSTRAINT FK2_EMP_MGR;
Table altered.
```

PK & FK Constraints

```
SQL> @cons
Enter value for table: emp
CONSTRAINT_NAME   TYPE   SEARCH_CONDITION     STATUS
---------------   ----   ----------------     -------
SYS_C006908       C      EMPNO IS NOT NULL    ENABLED
PK_EMP_EMPNO      P                           ENABLED
FK1_EMP_DEPTNO    R                           ENABLED
FK2_EMP_MGR       R                           ENABLED
Had to re-create the FK2_EMP_MGR FK constraint.
A quick note on the CONSTRAINT_TYPE column of
USER_CONSTRAINTS, ALL_CONSTRAINTS, and DBA_CONSTRAINTS.
```

```
CONSTRAINT_TYPE     Equivalent
---------------     ----------
P                   PRIMARY KEY
R                   FOREIGN KEY (Referential Integrity)
U                   UNIQUE
C                   CHECK
C                   NOT NULL
```

```
SQL> @are
Enter value for owner: student15
Enter value for table: emp
INDEX_NAME           TABLESPACE_NAME          UNIQUENES
-----------          ---------------          ---------
PK_EMP_EMPNO         USER_INDEX               UNIQUE
```

```
SQL> ALTER TABLE EMP DISABLE PRIMARY KEY;
ALTER TABLE EMP
*
ERROR at line 1:
ORA-02297:cannot disable constraint (STUDENT15.PK_EMP_EMPNO)
- dependencies exist
REMEMBER THE MGR COLUMN? IT DEPENDS UPON EMPNO OF EMP.
```

```
SQL> ALTER TABLE EMP DISABLE CONSTRAINT FK2_EMP_MGR;
Table altered.
```

```
SQL> ALTER TABLE EMP DISABLE PRIMARY KEY;
Table altered.
```

(Continued)

Let's examine the status of the constraints and indexes on the EMP table after you disable one of the FOREIGN KEY constraints, and the PRIMARY KEY constraint.

```
SQL> @cons
Enter value for table: emp
CONSTRAINT_NAME     TYPE    SEARCH_CONDITION        STATUS
---------------     ----    ----------------        --------
SYS_C006908         C       EMPNO IS NOT NULL       ENABLED
PK_EMP_EMPNO        P                               DISABLED
FK1_EMP_DEPTNO      R                               ENABLED
FK2_EMP_MGR         R                               DISABLED
```

When a PRIMARY KEY constraint has a status of "DISABLED", the unique index for the PK has been DELETED. When you enable the PK constraint, the unique index is re-created. If you are working with a large table, this requires some time.

```
SQL> @are
Enter value for owner: student15
Enter value for table: emp
no rows selected
```
See, no indexes on the EMP table now.
Hmm....Wonder if it matters which one(PK or FK) is enabled first?
```
SQL> ALTER TABLE EMP ENABLE CONSTRAINT FK2_EMP_MGR;
ALTER TABLE EMP ENABLE CONSTRAINT FK2_EMP_MGR
*
ERROR at line 1:
ORA-02270: no matching unique or primary key for this
column-list
```
YEP, SURE DOES!

```
SQL> ALTER TABLE EMP ENABLE CONSTRAINT PK_EMP_EMPNO;
Table altered.
SQL> ALTER TABLE EMP ENABLE PRIMARY KEY;
Either one of the above two commands accomplishes the same.
```

```
SQL> ALTER TABLE EMP ENABLE CONSTRAINT FK2_EMP_MGR;
Table altered.
```

PK Constraint "GOTCHA"

```
SQL> @cons
Enter value for table: emp
```

CONSTRAINT_NAME	TYPE	SEARCH_CONDITION	STATUS
SYS_C006908	C	EMPNO IS NOT NULL	ENABLED
PK_EMP_EMPNO	P		ENABLED
FK1_EMP_DEPTNO	R		ENABLED
FK2_EMP_MGR	R		ENABLED

```
SQL> @are
Enter value for owner: student15
Enter value for table: emp
```

INDEX_NAME	TABLESPACE_NAME	UNIQUENES
PK_EMP_EMPNO	USER_DATA	UNIQUE

Beware of just an ordinary ENABLE of a primary key constraint. You can see the unique index is placed in the same tablespace as the data, and you don't want that, if you want your database to perform as fast as possible.

```
SQL> ALTER TABLE EMP DISABLE CONSTRAINT FK2_EMP_MGR;
Table altered.

SQL> ALTER TABLE EMP DISABLE PRIMARY KEY;
Table altered.

SQL> ALTER TABLE EMP
  2         ENABLE PRIMARY KEY
  3         USING  INDEX    /* Best 2 Sep Data From Index */
  4         TABLESPACE USER_INDEX;
Table altered.

SQL> @are
Enter value for owner: student15
Enter value for table: emp
```

INDEX_NAME	TABLESPACE_NAME	UNIQUENES
PK_EMP_EMPNO	USER_INDEX	UNIQUE

Creating Foreign Key Constraints

The EMP table has two FOREIGN KEYS. One is on the DEPTNO column, since a ONE TO MANY relationship exists between DEPT and EMP. i.e. A department may be comprised of one or more employees, and an employee may be assigned to one and only one department according to our ERD model.

The second foreign key on the EMP table is a RECURSIVE foreign key. That is, EMP has a ONE TO MANY relationship with itself. i.e. An employee may be the manager of one or more employees, and an employee may be assigned to one and only one employee. This is a ONE TO MANY RECURSIVE relationship. And, the way a ONE TO MANY relationship is implemented at the table level, is to "GO WITH THE MANY". i.e. Take the PK pf the ONE, and place it as a FK in the MANY. That is the reason DEPTNO and MGR are columns in the EMP table, because of the 1:M relationships.

```
SQL> ALTER TABLE EMP
  2       ADD    CONSTRAINT FK1_EMP_DEPTNO
  3       FOREIGN KEY(DEPTNO)
  4       REFERENCES DEPT(DEPTNO);
Table altered.

SQL> ALTER TABLE EMP
  2       ADD    CONSTRAINT FK2_EMP_MGR
  3       FOREIGN KEY(MGR)
  4       REFERENCES EMP(EMPNO);
Table altered.
SQL> SELECT CONSTRAINT_NAME,
  2       CONSTRAINT_TYPE,   /* R=Referential Integrity */
  3       SEARCH_CONDITION,
  4       STATUS
  5  FROM   USER_CONSTRAINTS
  6* WHERE  TABLE_NAME       = UPPER('&Table') AND
         CONSTRAINT_TYPE = 'R';

Enter value for table: emp
CONSTRAINT_NAME    TYPE  SEARCH_CONDITION    STATUS
---------------    ----  ---------------    -------
FK1_EMP_DEPTNO      R                         ENABLED
FK2_EMP_MGR         R                         ENABLED
```

Implementing Cascade Deletes

Let's say every time you delete a department, you want to see all employees in the department deleted as well.

```
SQL> INSERT INTO DEPT VALUES(99, 'ART', 'TULSA');
1 row created.
SQL> INSERT INTO EMP(EMPNO,DEPTNO,ENAME)
  2        VALUES(1944, 99, 'PEDRO');
1 row created.
SQL> INSERT INTO EMP(EMPNO,DEPTNO,ENAME)
          VALUES(1950, 99, 'RUTH');
1 row created.
```

Now, let's see what happens when you try to enter a bogus department number - like 88.

```
SQL> INSERT INTO EMP(EMPNO, DEPTNO, ENAME)
          VALUES(1976, 88, 'PAIGE');
INSERT INTO EMP(EMPNO,DEPTNO,ENAME)
               *
ERROR at line 1:
ORA-02291: integrity constraint (STUDENT15.FK1_EMP_DEPTNO)
violated - parent key not found

SQL> SELECT ENAME, EMP.DEPTNO, LOC
  2  FROM    EMP,   DEPT
  3  WHERE   EMP.DEPTNO = DEPT.DEPTNO AND EMP.DEPTNO = 99;
ENAME          DEPTNO LOC
---------- ------- -------------
PEDRO              99 TULSA
RUTH               99 TULSA
SQL> ALTER TABLE EMP DROP CONSTRAINT FK1_EMP_DEPTNO;
Table altered.
SQL> ALTER TABLE EMP ADD CONSTRAINT FK1_EMP_DEPTNO
  2        FOREIGN KEY(DEPTNO) REFERENCES DEPT(DEPTNO)
  3        ON DELETE CASCADE;
Table altered.
SQL> DELETE FROM DEPT WHERE DEPTNO = 99;
1 row deleted.
SQL> SELECT ENAME, EMP.DEPTNO, LOC
  2  FROM    EMP,   DEPT
  3* WHERE   EMP.DEPTNO = DEPT.DEPTNO AND EMP.DEPTNO = 99;
no rows selected.
```

Creating Unique Constraints

All constraints can be included in the create table command with some restrictions. (PK's created befor FK's)

```
SQL> ALTER TABLE      DEPT
  2          ADD       CONSTRAINT UN_DEPT_LOC
  3          UNIQUE    (LOC)
  4          USING     INDEX
  5          TABLESPACE USER_INDEX
  6*         STORAGE   (INITIAL 2K    NEXT 2K)
SQL> /
Table altered.
```

```
SQL> @cons
Enter value for table: dept
CONSTRAINT_NAME       TYPE    SEARCH_CONDITION       STATUS
---------------       ----    ----------------       -------
PK_DEPT_DEPTNO        P                              ENABLED
UN_DEPT_LOC           U                              ENABLED
SQL> @are
Enter value for owner: student15
Enter value for table: dept
INDEX_NAME            TABLESPACE_NAME        UNIQUENES
--------------        ---------------        ---------
PK_DEPT_DEPTNO        USER_INDEX             UNIQUE
UN_DEPT_LOC           USER_INDEX             UNIQUE
```

```
SQL> UPDATE DEPT SET LOC = 'DALLAS' WHERE DEPTNO = 10;
UPDATE DEPT SET LOC = 'DALLAS' WHERE DEPTNO = 10
        *
ERROR at line 1:
ORA-00001: unique constraint (STUDENT15.UN_DEPT_LOC)
violated
```

```
SQL> ALTER TABLE DEPT DISABLE CONSTRAINT UN_DEPT_LOC;
Table altered.
SQL> @are
Enter value for owner: student15
Enter value for table: dept
INDEX_NAME            TABLESPACE_NAME        UNIQUENES
--------------        ---------------        ---------
PK_DEPT_DEPTNO        USER_INDEX             UNIQUE
```

Creating Check Constraints

```
SQL> ALTER TABLE EMP
  2         ADD   CONSTRAINT  CK_EMP_SAL_RANGE
  3         CHECK(SAL BETWEEN 500 AND 5500);
```
Table altered.
SQL> @cons
Enter value for table: **emp**

CONSTRAINT_NAME	TYPE	SEARCH_CONDITION	STATUS
SYS_C006908	C	EMPNO IS NOT NULL	ENABLED
PK_EMP_EMPNO	P		ENABLED
FK1_EMP_DEPTNO	R		ENABLED
CK_EMP_SAL_RANGE	**C**	**SAL BETWEEN 500 AND 5500**	**ENABLED**

SQL> UPDATE EMP SET SAL = 7000 WHERE ENAME = 'FORD';
UPDATE EMP
ERROR at line 1:
ORA-02290: check constraint (STUDENT15.CK_EMP_SAL_RANGE)
violated
SQL> ALTER TABLE EMP DISABLE CONSTRAINT CK_EMP_SAL_RANGE;
Table altered.
SQL> UPDATE EMP SET SAL = 7000 WHERE ENAME = 'FORD';
1 row updated.
SQL> ALTER TABLE EMP ENABLE CONSTRAINT CK_EMP_SAL_RANGE;
ALTER TABLE EMP ENABLE CONSTRAINT CK_EMP_SAL_RANGE
ERROR at line 1:
ORA-02296: cannot enable constraint
(STUDENT15.CK_EMP_SAL_RANGE) - found
noncomplying values
SQL> ALTER TABLE EMP ENABLE CONSTRAINT CK_EMP_SAL_RANGE
** 2   EXCEPTIONS INTO EXCEPTIONS;**
ALTER TABLE EMP ENABLE CONSTRAINT CK_EMP_SAL_RANGE
ERROR at line 1:
ORA-02296: cannot enable constraint
(STUDENT15.CK_EMP_SAL_RANGE) - found
noncomplying values
SQL> SELECT * FROM EXCEPTIONS;

ROW_ID	OWNER	TABLE_NAME	CONSTRAINT
00000263.000C.0006	STUDENT15	EMP	CK_EMP_SAL_RANGE

SQL> SELECT EMPNO,   ENAME
** 2 FROM   EMP,   EXCEPTIONS**
** 3 WHERE   EMP.ROWID = EXCEPTIONS.ROW_ID;**

EMPNO	ENAME
7902	FORD

Creating Not Null Constraints

```
SQL> ALTER TABLE       EMP
  2         MODIFY      SAL
  3         CONSTRAINT  NN_EMP_SAL
  4         NOT         NULL;
```
Table altered.

Yes, you may have more than one constraint on a column.

SQL> @cons
Enter value for table: **emp**

CONSTRAINT_NAME	TYPE	SEARCH_CONDITION	STATUS
SYS_C006908	C	EMPNO IS NOT NULL	ENABLED
PK_EMP_EMPNO	P		ENABLED
FK1_EMP_DEPTNO	R		ENABLED
CK_EMP_SAL_RANGE	**C**	**SAL BETWEEN 500 AND 5500**	**DISABLED**
NN_EMP_SAL	**C**	**SAL IS NOT NULL**	**ENABLED**

SQL> DESC EMP

Name	Null?	Type
EMPNO	NOT NULL	NUMBER(4)
ENAME		VARCHAR2(10)
JOB		VARCHAR2(9)
MGR		NUMBER(4)
HIREDATE		DATE
SAL	**NOT NULL**	**NUMBER(7,2)**
COMM		NUMBER(7,2)
DEPTNO		NUMBER(2)

Before you may change a column to NOT NULL, every row must have a value in that column, or you receive the following error message.

SQL> ALTER TABLE EMP
```
  2         MODIFY COMM
  3         CONSTRAINT NN_EMP_COMM
  4         NOT NULL;
```
MODIFY COMM
       *

ERROR at line 2:
ORA-01449:column contains NULL values;cannot alter to NOT NULL

Dropping NOT NULL Constraints

```
SQL> DESC EMP
 Name                                   Null?    Type
 -------------------------------------- -------- ----
 EMPNO                                  NOT NULL NUMBER(4)
 ENAME                                           VARCHAR2(10)
 JOB                                             VARCHAR2(9)
 MGR                                             NUMBER(4)
 HIREDATE                                        DATE
 SAL                                    NOT NULL NUMBER(7,2)
 COMM                                            NUMBER(7,2)
 DEPTNO                                          NUMBER(2)
```

```
SQL> ALTER TABLE EMP DROP CONSTRAINT NN_EMP_SAL;
```

Table altered.

```
SQL> DESC EMP
 Name                                   Null?    Type
 -------------------------------------- -------- ----
 EMPNO                                  NOT NULL NUMBER(4)
 ENAME                                           VARCHAR2(10)
 JOB                                             VARCHAR2(9)
 MGR                                             NUMBER(4)
 HIREDATE                                        DATE
 SAL                                             NUMBER(7,2)
 COMM                                            NUMBER(7,2)
 DEPTNO                                          NUMBER(2)
```

Renaming SYS_C999999 Constraints

```
SQL> ALTER TABLE EMP
  2         MODIFY SAL NOT NULL;
Table altered.

SQL> DESC EMP
 Name                                  Null?    Type
 ------------------------------------- -------- ----
SAL                                   NOT NULL NUMBER(7,2)
Not interested in the other columns, so I cut them out here.

SQL> @cons
Enter value for table: emp
CONSTRAINT_NAME      TYPE  SEARCH_CONDITION               STATUS
---------------      ----  --------------------------     --------
SYS_C006908          C     EMPNO IS NOT NULL              ENABLED
PK_EMP_EMPNO         P                                    ENABLED
FK1_EMP_DEPTNO       R                                    ENABLED
CK_EMP_SAL_RANGE     C     SAL BETWEEN 500 AND 5500       DISABLED
SYS_C006921          C     SAL IS NOT NULL                ENABLED

SQL> ALTER TABLE EMP DROP CONSTRAINT SYS_C006921;
Table altered.

SQL> ALTER TABLE EMP
  2         MODIFY  SAL
  3         CONSTRAINT NN_EMP_SAL
  4         NOT NULL;
Table altered.

SQL> SELECT CONSTRAINT_NAME,
  2         CONSTRAINT_TYPE,
  3         SEARCH_CONDITION,
  4         STATUS
  5  FROM   USER_CONSTRAINTS
  6* WHERE  TABLE_NAME = 'EMP' AND CONSTRAINT_TYPE = 'C'
SQL> /
CONSTRAINT_NAME   TYPE  SEARCH_CONDITION          STATUS
---------------   ----  ----------------          --------
SYS_C006908       C     EMPNO IS NOT NULL         ENABLED
CK_EMP_SAL_RANGE  C     SAL BETWEEN 500 AND 5500  DISABLED
NN_EMP_SAL        C     SAL IS NOT NULL           ENABLED
```

Renaming Tables

```
SQL> RENAME DEPT TO D1;

Table renamed.

SQL> UPDATE EMP
  2  SET     DEPTNO  = 44
  3  WHERE   ENAME   = 'FORD';
UPDATE EMP
       *
ERROR at line 1:
ORA-02291: integrity constraint (STUDENT15.FK1_EMP_DEPTNO)
violated - parent
key not found
```

Yes, the constraints follow a table when it is renamed.

Implementing Social Security Format Using Constraints

```
SQL> ALTER TABLE EMP
  2         ADD    SSN    VARCHAR2(11);

Table altered.

SQL> DESC EMP
 Name                                    Null?     Type
 ------------------------------------ -------- ----
 EMPNO                                NOT NULL NUMBER(4)
 ENAME                                         VARCHAR2(10)
 JOB                                           VARCHAR2(9)
 MGR                                           NUMBER(4)
 HIREDATE                                      DATE
 SAL                                  NOT NULL NUMBER(7,2)
 COMM                                          NUMBER(7,2)
 DEPTNO                                        NUMBER(2)
 SSN                                           VARCHAR2(11)

SQL>  ALTER TABLE EMP
  2    ADD    CONSTRAINT  CK_EMP_SSN
  3    CHECK(TRANSLATE(SSN,'0123456789-',
  4*                   '9999999999D') = '999D99D9999');
Table altered.

SQL> UPDATE EMP
  2   SET    SSN   = '123-45-6789'
  3   WHERE  ENAME = 'FORD';
1 rows updated.

SQL> UPDATE EMP
  2   SET    SSN   = '12-345-6789'
  3   WHERE  ENAME = 'FORD';
WHERE   ENAME = 'FORD'
                     *
ERROR at line 3:
ORA-02290: check constraint (STUDENT15.CK_EMP_SSN) violated
```

> If two wrongs don't make a right, and two rights
> don't make a wrong, then what do two rights make?
> Answer: An airplane. (Orville And Wilbur Wright)

CHAPTER

7

Before Dinner
Appetizer
Or
Set Operators

Avoiding Pitfalls When Using Set Operators

```
SQL> SELECT DEPTNO FROM EMP
  2  UNION
  3  SELECT LOC     FROM DEPT;
SELECT DEPTNO FROM EMP
       *
ERROR at line 1:
ORA-01790: expression must have same datatype as
corresponding expression
```

```
SQL> SELECT DEPTNO FROM EMP
  2  UNION
  3* SELECT DEPTNO, LOC FROM DEPT;

SELECT DEPTNO FROM EMP
*
ERROR at line 1:
ORA-01789: query block has incorrect number of result
columns
```

```
SQL> SELECT DEPTNO FROM EMP   /* SAME #COLS & DATA TYPES */
  2  UNION                    /* DEPTNO'S IN EITHER       */
  3  SELECT DEPTNO FROM DEPT;

 DEPTNO
-------
     10
     20
     30
     40
     99
```

Displaying The Lyrics Of A Song Using Union

```
SQL> SELECT 9 DUMMY, 'Was Blind, But Now I See' FROM DUAL;
  DUMMY 'WASBLIND,BUTNOWISEE'
------- -----------------------------
      9 Was Blind, But Now I See
SQL> l
  1  SELECT 9 DUMMY, 'Was Blind, But Now I See' FROM DUAL
  2  UNION
  3* SELECT 1 DUMMY, 'Amazing Grace, How Sweet The Sound'
     FROM      DUAL
SQL> /
  DUMMY 'WASBLIND,BUTNOWISEE'
------- -----------------------------------
      1 Amazing Grace, How Sweet The Sound
      9 Was Blind, But Now I See
SQL> SELECT 9 DUMMY, 'Was Blind, But Now I See' FROM DUAL
  2  UNION
  3  SELECT 1 DUMMY, 'Amazing Grace, How Sweet The Sound'
  4  FROM      DUAL
  5  UNION
  6* SELECT 5 DUMMY,'That Saved A Wretch Like Me' FROM DUAL;
  DUMMY 'WASBLIND,BUTNOWISEE'
------- -----------------------------------
      1 Amazing Grace, How Sweet The Sound
      5 That Saved A Wretch Like Me
      9 Was Blind, But Now I See
SQL> SELECT 9 DUMMY, 'Was Blind, But Now I See' FROM DUAL
  2  UNION
  3  SELECT 1 DUMMY, 'Amazing Grace, How Sweet The Sound'
  4  FROM      DUAL
  5  UNION
  6  SELECT 5 DUMMY, 'That Saved A Wretch Like Me' FROM DUAL
  7  UNION
  8  SELECT 7 DUMMY, 'I Once Was Lost, But Now Am Found'
  9* FROM      DUAL;
  DUMMY 'WASBLIND,BUTNOWISEE'
------- -----------------------------------
      1 Amazing Grace, How Sweet The Sound
      5 That Saved A Wretch Like Me
      7 I Once Was Lost, But Now Am Found
      9 Was Blind, But Now I See
```

(Continued)

```
SQL> SET HEADING OFF
SQL> /
     1 Amazing Grace, How Sweet The Sound
     5 That Saved A Wretch Like Me
     7 I Once Was Lost, But Now Am Found
     9 Was Blind, But Now I See
SQL> COL DUMMY NOPRINT
SQL> /
Amazing Grace, How Sweet The Sound
That Saved A Wretch Like Me
I Once Was Lost, But Now Am Found
Was Blind, But Now I See
```

It's smarter to place all of these commands in a script file.

```
SQL> get cb290
  1   SET      HEADING     OFF
  2   COL      DUMMY       NOPRINT
  3   SELECT 9 DUMMY, 'Was Blind, But Now I See' FROM DUAL
  4   UNION
  5   SELECT 1 DUMMY, 'Amazing Grace, How Sweet The Sound'
  6   FROM     DUAL
  7   UNION
  8   SELECT 5 DUMMY, 'That Saved A Wretch Like Me' FROM DUAL
  9   UNION
 10   SELECT 7 DUMMY, 'I Once Was Lost, But Now Am Found'
 11   FROM     DUAL
 12   /
 13   SET      HEADING     ON
 14*  COL      DUMMY       PRINT

SQL> @cb290
Amazing Grace, How Sweet The Sound
That Saved A Wretch Like Me
I Once Was Lost, But Now Am Found
Was Blind, But Now I See
```

UNION In A Report

```
SQL> get cb291
  1   SET HEADING   OFF
  2   COL DEPTNO    NOPRINT
  3   COL RPT_TYPE NOPRINT
  4   SET LINESIZE 44
  5   SET PAGESIZE 66
  6   SET ECHO      OFF
  7   SET FEEDBACK OFF
  8   SPOOL REPORT.lis
  9   SELECT DEPTNO, 0 RPT_TYPE,
 10          RPAD('Department:  ' || DNAME, 44) ||
 11          RPAD('---------------------', 44)
 12   FROM    DEPT
 13   WHERE   DEPTNO IN(SELECT DISTINCT DEPTNO FROM EMP)
 14   UNION
 15   SELECT DEPTNO, 5 RPT_TYPE, '      ' || RPAD(ENAME,10) ||
 16          LPAD(TO_CHAR(SAL,'$99,999.99'),30)
 17   FROM    EMP
 18   UNION
 19   SELECT DEPTNO,7 RPT_TYPE, LPAD('---------------',44) ||
 20          LPAD(TO_CHAR(SUM(SAL),'$999,999.99'),44)        ||
 21          LPAD('==============',44)
 22   FROM    EMP
 23   GROUP BY DEPTNO
 24   ORDER BY 1,2
 25   /
 26   SPOOL   OFF
 27   SET     HEADING   ON
 28   COL     DEPTNO    PRINT
 29   SET     LINESIZE 80
 30   SET     PAGESIZE 24
 31   SET     FEEDBACK ON
 32*  SET     ECHO      ON
SQL> @cb291
Department:  ACCOUNTING
---------------------
    CLARK                          $2,450.00
    KING                           $5,000.00
    MILLER                         $1,300.00
                                   ---------------
                                   $8,750.00
                                   ==============
```

Observing All Database Files Using Union

```
SQL> @cb294
SQL> SELECT  SUBSTR(NAME,    1, 55) "Database Files"
  2  FROM    V$DBFILE
  3  UNION
  4  SELECT  SUBSTR(MEMBER, 1, 55) "Database Files"
  5  FROM    V$LOGFILE
  6  UNION
  7  SELECT  SUBSTR(NAME,    1, 55) "Database Files"
  8  FROM    V$CONTROLFILE
  9  /
```

```
Database Files
---------------------------------------------------------
/home2/oracle/7.1.3/dbs/ctrl1ora713.ctl
/home2/oracle/7.1.3/dbs/ctrl2ora713.ctl
/home2/oracle/7.1.3/dbs/ctrl3ora713.ctl
/home2/oracle/7.1.3/dbs/log1ora713.dbf
/home2/oracle/7.1.3/dbs/log2ora713.dbf
/home2/oracle/7.1.3/dbs/log3ora713.dbf
/home2/oracle/7.1.3/dbs/rbsora713.dbf
/home2/oracle/7.1.3/dbs/rbsora713_2.dbf
/home2/oracle/7.1.3/dbs/read_only.dbf
/home2/oracle/7.1.3/dbs/user_data.dbf
/home2/oracle/7.1.3/dbs/user_idx.dbf
/home2/oracle/7.1.3/dbs/systora713.dbf
/home2/oracle/7.1.3/dbs/systora713_2.dbf
/home2/oracle/7.1.3/dbs/systora713_3.dbf
/home2/oracle/7.1.3/dbs/tempora713.dbf
/home2/oracle/7.1.3/dbs/tool2ora713.dbf
/home2/oracle/7.1.3/dbs/toolora713.dbf
/home2/oracle/7.1.3/dbs/usersora713.dbf
/home3/ora713/dbs/des2_rbs.dbf

24 rows selected.
```

Using Intersect

What departments have at least one employee ?

Method 1:
SQL> SELECT DEPTNO FROM EMP
  2 INTERSECT
  3 SELECT DEPTNO FROM DEPT;

```
 DEPTNO
-------
     10
     20
     30
```

3 rows selected.

Method 2:
SQL> SELECT ENAME, LOC, DEPT.DEPTNO
  2 FROM   EMP,   DEPT
  3 WHERE EMP.DEPTNO = DEPT.DEPTNO;

```
ENAME        LOC            DEPTNO
----------   -------------  -------
CLARK        NEW YORK            10
KING         NEW YORK            10
MILLER       NEW YORK            10
SMITH        DALLAS              20
ADAMS        DALLAS              20
FORD         DALLAS              20
SCOTT        DALLAS              20
JONES        DALLAS              20
ALLEN        CHICAGO             30
BLAKE        CHICAGO             30
MARTIN       CHICAGO             30
JAMES        CHICAGO             30
BIG BUCKS    CHICAGO             30
PAIGE        CHICAGO             30
TURNER       CHICAGO             30
WARD         CHICAGO             30
```

16 rows selected.

Using Minus

A bank has around 9,000,000 rows in the checking account table, but only 2,000,000 rows in the savings account table. A correlated sub-query works, but it requires around seventy hours to run. It looks something like this:

```
SQL> SELECT  CNAME                    -- We Are Talking Slow Here
     FROM    CHECKING
     WHERE   NOT EXISTS (SELECT 'X'
                  FROM     SAVINGS
                  WHERE    CHECKING.CNAME = SAVINGS.CNAME);
```

How does five hours sound compared to seventy hours ?

```
SQL> SELECT  CNAME FROM CHECKING
     MINUS
     SELECT  SNAME FROM SAVINGS;
```

CHAPTER

8

*Soup Of The
Day (Soup de Jour)
Or
Five Types
Of Joins*

The Horrible Join

```
SQL> SELECT ENAME, DEPTNO
  2  FROM    EMP
  3  ORDER   BY DEPTNO;

ENAME       DEPTNO
---------- -------
CLARK          10
KING           10
MILLER         10
SMITH          20
ADAMS          20
FORD           20
SCOTT          20
JONES          20
ALLEN          30
BLAKE          30
MARTIN         30
JAMES          30
TURNER         30
WARD           30
PAIGE          88 (Referential Integ. Constraint Disabled)

15 rows selected.
```

> Here today, gone to MAUI.
> Happily MAUIED.
> MAUI Christmas.
> Don't worry, be MAUI.
> You go your way, I'll go MAUI.
> What ? Me MAUI ?

```
SQL> SELECT *
  2  FROM    DEPT
  3  ORDER   BY DEPTNO;

 DEPTNO DNAME          LOC
------- -------------- -------------
     10 ACCOUNTING     NEW YORK
     20 RESEARCH       DALLAS
     30 SALES          CHICAGO
     40 OPERATIONS     BOSTON     (Empty department)
     99 MIS            MAUI       (Empty department)
```

Results Of A Join With No "WHERE" Clause

Paige is in a non-existant department(88), and departments
40 and 99 do not have any employees in them.
Throughout the next few pages, the goal is to retrieve all
of the employee names, including Paige, and all of the
department locations, including Boston and Maui. By
omitting the join part of the "WHERE" clause,
WHERE EMP.DEPTNO = DEPT.DEPTNO, you produce the Cartesian
product of the two tables. And, since each employee would
work in all locations, the active set is 15 X 5 = 75 rows.
Fifteen employees times five departments equals seventy five
possible permutations. That is why the WHERE ENAME IN
clause is used here to reduce the active set to something
you can see on one page. Notice all three employees seem to
be working in all locations. (NOT !!) So, the example
consists of three employees working in perhaps five
departments which produces fifteen rows in the active set.

(3 X 5 = 15)

```
SQL> SELECT  ENAME,  LOC
  2  FROM    EMP,   DEPT
  3* WHERE   ENAME IN('ADAMS', 'FORD', 'PAIGE');
```

```
ENAME       LOC
----------  -------------
ADAMS       NEW YORK
FORD        NEW YORK
PAIGE       NEW YORK
ADAMS       DALLAS
FORD        DALLAS
PAIGE       DALLAS
ADAMS       CHICAGO
FORD        CHICAGO
PAIGE       CHICAGO
ADAMS       BOSTON
FORD        BOSTON
PAIGE       BOSTON
ADAMS       MAUI
FORD        MAUI
PAIGE       MAUI
```

15 rows selected.

Deliberate Omission Of "WHERE"Clause When Joining

```
SQL> CREATE TABLE SINGLE_FEMALES
  2          (FNAME    VARCHAR2(20))
  3*         STORAGE(INITIAL 2K    NEXT 2K)
SQL> /

Table created.

SQL> get cb307
  1  CREATE TABLE SINGLE_MALES
  2          (MNAME    VARCHAR2(20))
  3*         STORAGE(INITIAL 2K    NEXT 2K)
SQL> /

Table created.


SQL> set feedback off


SQL> set echo off


SQL> @cb308


SQL> get cb308
  1  INSERT INTO SINGLE_FEMALES VALUES('LE PYOU');
  2  INSERT INTO SINGLE_FEMALES VALUES('ANN HARDLY');
  3  INSERT INTO SINGLE_FEMALES VALUES('ANN ALLIE');
  4  INSERT INTO SINGLE_MALES   VALUES('LAUREL');
  5  INSERT INTO SINGLE_MALES   VALUES('KUPEL FRAN');
  6  INSERT INTO SINGLE_MALES   VALUES('PIERRE');
  7* COMMIT;
```

(Continued)

```
SQL> get cb309
  1   SET     HEADING         OFF
  2   SET     FEEDBACK        OFF
  3   SELECT MNAME || ' ' || FNAME
  4   FROM    SINGLE_MALES,   SINGLE_FEMALES
  5   /
  6   SET     HEADING         ON
  7*  SET     FEEDBACK        ON

SQL> @cb309

LAUREL LE PYOU
KUPEL FRAN LE PYOU
PIERRE LE PYOU
LAUREL ANN HARDLY
KUPEL FRAN ANN HARDLY
PIERRE ANN HARDLY
LAUREL ANN ALLIE
KUPEL FRAN ANN ALLIE
PIERRE ANN ALLIE

SQL> SET     HEADING         ON
SQL> SET     FEEDBACK        ON
```

Writing A Simple/Inner/Equal Join

```
SQL> SELECT * FROM DEPT;
 DEPTNO DNAME          LOC
 ------- -------------- -------------
     10 ACCOUNTING     NEW YORK
     20 RESEARCH       DALLAS
     30 SALES          CHICAGO
     40 OPERATIONS     BOSTON
     99 MIS            MAUI
5 rows selected.

SQL> SELECT ENAME, DEPTNO  /* Emp's With Bogus Deptno's  */
  2  FROM    EMP
  3  WHERE   DEPTNO NOT IN(SELECT DEPTNO FROM DEPT);
ENAME       DEPTNO
---------- -------
PAIGE           88
1 row selected.

SQL> get cb310
  1  SELECT ENAME, LOC /* Where Is Paige,Boston,And Maui? */
  2  FROM    EMP,   DEPT
  3* WHERE   EMP.DEPTNO = DEPT.DEPTNO
SQL> /
ENAME       LOC
---------- -------------

CLARK       NEW YORK
KING        NEW YORK
MILLER      NEW YORK
SMITH       DALLAS
ADAMS       DALLAS
FORD        DALLAS
SCOTT       DALLAS
JONES       DALLAS
ALLEN       CHICAGO
BLAKE       CHICAGO
MARTIN      CHICAGO
JAMES       CHICAGO
TURNER      CHICAGO
WARD        CHICAGO

14 rows selected.
```

Correcting Column Ambiguously Defined Error

```
SQL> SELECT  ENAME, LOC, DEPTNO   /*  I'm Sooo Confused !!! */
  2  FROM    EMP,   DEPT           /*  Confused = Ambiguous  */
  3* WHERE   EMP.DEPTNO = DEPT.DEPTNO;

SELECT ENAME, LOC, DEPTNO   /*  I'm Sooo Confused !!! */
                   *
ERROR at line 1:
ORA-00918: column ambiguously defined
```

Do you mean DEPTNO from the EMP table, or DEPTNO from the
DEPT table. Oracle is great, but it is not into mind
reading yet.

```
SQL> SELECT  ENAME, LOC, EMP.DEPTNO   /* No Longer Confused */
  2  FROM    EMP,   DEPT
  3* WHERE   EMP.DEPTNO = DEPT.DEPTNO;

ENAME        LOC            DEPTNO
----------   -------------  -------
CLARK        NEW YORK           10
KING         NEW YORK           10
MILLER       NEW YORK           10
SMITH        DALLAS             20
ADAMS        DALLAS             20
FORD         DALLAS             20
SCOTT        DALLAS             20
JONES        DALLAS             20
ALLEN        CHICAGO            30
BLAKE        CHICAGO            30
MARTIN       CHICAGO            30
JAMES        CHICAGO            30
TURNER       CHICAGO            30
WARD         CHICAGO            30
14 rows selected.

SQL> SELECT  ENAME,LOC,DEPT.DEPTNO
  2  FROM    EMP,   DEPT   /* Either Way, I'm Not Confused */
  3* WHERE   EMP.DEPTNO = DEPT.DEPTNO;
```

Writing An Outer-Join (+)

```
SQL> SELECT  ENAME, LOC /* Get Paige This Time As Well */
  2  FROM    EMP,    DEPT
  3* WHERE   EMP.DEPTNO = DEPT.DEPTNO(+);
```

```
ENAME        LOC
----------   -------------
CLARK        NEW YORK
KING         NEW YORK
MILLER       NEW YORK
SMITH        DALLAS
ADAMS        DALLAS
FORD         DALLAS
SCOTT        DALLAS
JONES        DALLAS
ALLEN        CHICAGO
BLAKE        CHICAGO
MARTIN       CHICAGO
JAMES        CHICAGO
TURNER       CHICAGO
WARD         CHICAGO
PAIGE

15 rows selected.
```

```
You can tell this is an OUTER-JOIN because of the "(+)"
in the WHERE clause.  This query causes a NULL ROW from the
DEPT table to be joined with PAIGE's row, even though
Paige's department number 88 does not find a match in the
DEPT table.  The table associated with the "(+)" contains
the NULL ROW.
```

(Continued)

```
SQL> SELECT ENAME, LOC    /* Get Boston And Maui */
  2  FROM    EMP,    DEPT
  3* WHERE   EMP.DEPTNO(+) = DEPT.DEPTNO;
ENAME      LOC
---------- -------------
CLARK      NEW YORK
KING       NEW YORK
MILLER     NEW YORK
SMITH      DALLAS
ADAMS      DALLAS
FORD       DALLAS
SCOTT      DALLAS
JONES      DALLAS
ALLEN      CHICAGO
BLAKE      CHICAGO
MARTIN     CHICAGO
JAMES      CHICAGO
TURNER     CHICAGO
WARD       CHICAGO
           BOSTON
           MAUI
16 rows selected.
```
Well, you are getting closer, but what happened to Paige ?
```
SQL> SELECT ENAME, LOC    /* Try (+) On Both Sides */
  2  FROM    EMP,    DEPT
  3* WHERE   EMP.DEPTNO(+) = DEPT.DEPTNO(+);
WHERE   EMP.DEPTNO(+) = DEPT.DEPTNO(+)
                              *

ERROR at line 3:
ORA-01468: a predicate may reference only one outer-joined
table
```
Nice try, but still no cigar.
```
SQL> SELECT ENAME, LOC    /* Try An "OR" */
  2  FROM    EMP,    DEPT
  3  WHERE   EMP.DEPTNO(+) = DEPT.DEPTNO OR
  4*         EMP.DEPTNO    = DEPT.DEPTNO(+);
EMP.DEPTNO    = DEPT.DEPTNO(+)
                      *

ERROR at line 4:
ORA-01719: outer join operator (+) not allowed in operand of
OR or IN
```

Retrieving All Rows From All Tables Joined (Get Em All)

```
SQL> SELECT  ENAME, LOC       /*  Get Em All  */
  2  FROM    EMP,    DEPT
  3  WHERE   EMP.DEPTNO    = DEPT.DEPTNO(+)
  4  UNION
  5  SELECT  ENAME, LOC
  6  FROM    EMP,    DEPT
  7* WHERE   EMP.DEPTNO(+) = DEPT.DEPTNO;
```

```
ENAME       LOC
---------- -------------
ADAMS       DALLAS
ALLEN       CHICAGO
BLAKE       CHICAGO
CLARK       NEW YORK
FORD        DALLAS
JAMES       CHICAGO
JONES       DALLAS
KING        NEW YORK
MARTIN      CHICAGO
MILLER      NEW YORK
PAIGE
SCOTT       DALLAS
SMITH       DALLAS
TURNER      CHICAGO
WARD        CHICAGO
            BOSTON
            MAUI

17 rows selected.
```

BOM Report Using Self-Join

```
SQL> SELECT *
  2  FROM   PARTS;


    PNO PNAME                 COMPONENT_OF
------- -------------------- ------------
      1 SPRINT CAR
      2 CHASSIS                         1
      3 AXLES                           2
      4 ENGINE                          2
      5 SKINS                           2
      6 DASH                            2
      7 OIL GAGE                        6
      8 TEMP GAGE                       6
      9 STEARING COLUMN                 2
     10 STEARING WHEEL                  9
     11 POP OFF DEVICE                 10
     12 WHEELS                          3
     13 WING                           14
     14 ROLL CAGE                       2
     15 BRAKES                          3
     16 FUEL CELL                       2
     17 SHUT OFF SWITCH                 6
     18 SEAT                           19
     19 FLOOR BOARD                     2
     20 FRONT WING                      2
     21 FUEL CAP                       16

21 rows selected.
```

The PARTS table is a very special table in that it is
RECURSIVE. The PRIMARY KEY is PNO, and the COMPONENT_OF
column is a FOREIGN KEY referencing the PNO column of the
same table. When this occurs in Oracle, you can write SELF
JOINS, SELF-OUTER-JOINS, and use the CONNECT BY and START
WITH clauses.

(Continued)

Let's write a BOM (Bill Of Materials) type of query.


```
SQL> SET      HEADING       OFF
  2   SELECT PARTS.PNAME || ' is a component of ' || C.PNAME
  3   FROM     PARTS,   PARTS C
  4   WHERE    PARTS.COMPONENT_OF = C.PNO
  5   /
  6*  SET      HEADING       ON
SQL> @cb317b
```


CHASSIS is a component of SPRINT CAR
AXLES is a component of CHASSIS
ENGINE is a component of CHASSIS
DASH is a component of CHASSIS
FUEL CELL is a component of CHASSIS
FRONT WING is a component of CHASSIS
FLOOR BOARD is a component of CHASSIS
ROLL CAGE is a component of CHASSIS
SKINS is a component of CHASSIS
STEARING COLUMN is a component of CHASSIS
WHEELS is a component of AXLES
BRAKES is a component of AXLES
OIL GAGE is a component of DASH
SHUT OFF SWITCH is a component of DASH
TEMP GAGE is a component of DASH
STEARING WHEEL is a component of STEARING COLUMN
POP OFF DEVICE is a component of STEARING WHEEL
WING is a component of ROLL CAGE
FUEL CAP is a component of FUEL CELL
SEAT is a component of FLOOR BOARD

20 rows selected.

Notice that one part is missing from the active set.
The **"SPRINT CAR"** !!!!

To return "SPRINT CAR", you need to be a little devious.

Retrieving Level 1 In A Self-Join Using (+) (Self-Outer-Join)

Since you are performing a "SELF-JOIN", and are using the
"(+)" symbol to indicate an "OUTER-JOIN", it follows you can
refer to this type of a query, as a "SELF-OUTER-JOIN".

```
SQL>  SET     HEADING     OFF
  2   SELECT PARTS.PNAME || ' is a component of ' || C.PNAME
  3   FROM    PARTS,   PARTS C
  4   WHERE   PARTS.COMPONENT_OF = C.PNO(+)
  5   /
  6*  SET     HEADING     ON
SQL>  @cb318
```

CHASSIS is a component of SPRINT CAR
AXLES is a component of CHASSIS
ENGINE is a component of CHASSIS
DASH is a component of CHASSIS
FUEL CELL is a component of CHASSIS
FRONT WING is a component of CHASSIS
FLOOR BOARD is a component of CHASSIS
ROLL CAGE is a component of CHASSIS
SKINS is a component of CHASSIS
STEARING COLUMN is a component of CHASSIS
WHEELS is a component of AXLES
BRAKES is a component of AXLES
OIL GAGE is a component of DASH
SHUT OFF SWITCH is a component of DASH
TEMP GAGE is a component of DASH
STEARING WHEEL is a component of STEARING COLUMN
POP OFF DEVICE is a component of STEARING WHEEL
WING is a component of ROLL CAGE
FUEL CAP is a component of FUEL CELL
SEAT is a component of FLOOR BOARD
SPRINT CAR is a component of

21 rows selected.

Using NVL In Self-Outer-Joins

```
SQL> SET     HEADING     OFF
  2   SELECT PARTS.PNAME ||' is a component of '||
NVL(C.PNAME, 'Nothing')
  3   FROM    PARTS,  PARTS C
  4   WHERE   PARTS.COMPONENT_OF = C.PNO(+)
  5   /
  6*  SET     HEADING     ON
SQL> @cb318
```

CHASSIS is a component of SPRINT CAR
AXLES is a component of CHASSIS
ENGINE is a component of CHASSIS
DASH is a component of CHASSIS
FUEL CELL is a component of CHASSIS
FRONT WING is a component of CHASSIS
FLOOR BOARD is a component of CHASSIS
ROLL CAGE is a component of CHASSIS
SKINS is a component of CHASSIS
STEARING COLUMN is a component of CHASSIS
WHEELS is a component of AXLES
BRAKES is a component of AXLES
OIL GAGE is a component of DASH
SHUT OFF SWITCH is a component of DASH
TEMP GAGE is a component of DASH
STEARING WHEEL is a component of STEARING COLUMN
POP OFF DEVICE is a component of STEARING WHEEL
WING is a component of ROLL CAGE
FUEL CAP is a component of FUEL CELL
SEAT is a component of FLOOR BOARD
SPRINT CAR is a component of Nothing

21 rows selected.

BOM Report Using "Connect By Prior" & "Start With"

```
SQL> COL      "Bill Of Materials"    FORMAT    A30
  2  SELECT   LPAD(' ', 3*LEVEL) || PNAME "Bill Of Materials"
  3  FROM     PARTS
  4  CONNECT BY PRIOR PNO = COMPONENT_OF
  5* START    WITH PNAME   = 'SPRINT CAR'
SQL> @cb319
```

```
Bill Of Materials
------------------------------
   SPRINT CAR
      CHASSIS
         AXLES
            WHEELS
            BRAKES
         ENGINE
         SKINS
         DASH
            OIL GAGE
            TEMP GAGE
            SHUT OFF SWITCH
         STEARING COLUMN
            STEARING WHEEL
               POP OFF DEVICE
         ROLL CAGE
            WING
         FUEL CELL
            FUEL CAP
         FLOOR BOARD
            SEAT
         FRONT WING

21 rows selected.
```

Here you are padding with SPACES to the left of the part name using the function "LPAD"(Left Pad), in conjunction with the PSEUDO column "LEVEL". SPRINT CAR is LEVEL 1, CHASSIS is LEVEL 2, AXLES, ENGINE, SKINS, DASH, STEARING COLUMN, ROLL CAGE, FUEL CELL, FLOOR BOARD, and FRONT WING are LEVEL 3.

Three Table Outer-Join

```
SQL> SELECT *
  2  FROM    HISTORY;
  DEPTNO DUDE
------- ----------------
     10 ROY ROGERS
     20 HOPPY
     30 JOHN WAYNE
     40 RANDOLPH SCOTT
4 rows selected.
SQL> SELECT DISTINCT DEPTNO FROM EMP;
 DEPTNO
-------
     10
     20
     30
     44              DEBRA IS IN DEPT 44
     77              PAIGE IS IN DEPT 77
5 rows selected.
SQL> SELECT ENAME, LOC, DUDE  -- To See Debra & Paige
  2  FROM    EMP E, DEPT D, HISTORY H  -- Must Do (+)
  3  WHERE   E.DEPTNO = D.DEPTNO(+) AND
  4*         D.DEPTNO = H.DEPTNO(+);
ENAME       LOC           DUDE
----------  ------------- ----------------

CLARK       NEW YORK      ROY ROGERS
KING        NEW YORK      ROY ROGERS
MILLER      NEW YORK      ROY ROGERS
SMITH       DALLAS        HOPPY
ADAMS       DALLAS        HOPPY
SCOTT       DALLAS        HOPPY
JONES       DALLAS        HOPPY
ALLEN       CHICAGO       JOHN WAYNE
BIG BUCKS   CHICAGO       JOHN WAYNE
BLAKE       CHICAGO       JOHN WAYNE
MARTIN      CHICAGO       JOHN WAYNE
JAMES       CHICAGO       JOHN WAYNE
TURNER      CHICAGO       JOHN WAYNE
WARD        CHICAGO       JOHN WAYNE
DEBRA
PAIGE
```

A Very Unique Self-Outer-Join

Using a SELF-JOIN, write a non-subquery returning the highest paid monthly salaried employee.

```
SQL> SELECT A.ENAME, A.SAL
  2  FROM    EMP A,   EMP B
  3  WHERE   A.SAL    < B.SAL(+) AND
  4*                    B.SAL IS NULL;
```

```
ENAME          SAL
---------- -------
KING          5000
```

CHAPTER

9

Main Course

Lobster (Du Homard)

Or

Subqueries

Writing Simple Subqueries

Blake seems to think he is underpaid.   What do you think?

```
SQL> get cb300
  1   INSERT INTO EMP(EMPNO,ENAME,JOB,HIREDATE,SAL,DEPTNO)
  2*  VALUES(8888,'BIG BUCKS','MANAGER','03-MAY-88',5500,30)
SQL> /

1 row created.


SQL> get cb301
  1   SELECT *
  2   FROM    EMP
  3   WHERE SAL>(SELECT SAL FROM EMP WHERE ENAME='BLAKE') AND
  4       JOB =(SELECT JOB FROM EMP WHERE ENAME= 'BLAKE') AND
  5*HIREDATE>(SELECT HIREDATE FROM EMP WHERE ENAME='BLAKE')
SQL> /
```

EMPNO	ENAME	JOB	MGR	HIREDATE	SAL	COMM	DEPTNO
8888	**BIG BUCKS**	MANAGER		03-MAY-88	5500		30

Writing Subqueries Using &

```
SQL> get cb302
  1  SELECT *
  2  FROM    EMP
  3  WHERE SAL>(SELECT SAL FROM EMP WHERE ENAME='&NAME') AND
  4    JOB = (SELECT JOB FROM EMP WHERE ENAME = '&NAME') AND
  5*HIREDATE>(SELECT HIREDATE FROM EMP WHERE ENAME='&NAME')
SQL> /

Enter value for name: BLAKE
Enter value for name: BLAKE
Enter value for name: BLAKE


EMPNO ENAME      JOB        MGR HIREDATE    SAL COMM DEPTNO
----- --------- ------- ---- --------- ---- ---- ------
8888  BIG BUCKS MANAGER      03-MAY-88 5500            30
```

Writing Subqueries Using && To Prompt Once

```
SQL> get cb302
  1   SELECT *
  2   FROM    EMP
  3   WHERE SAL>(SELECT SAL FROM EMP WHERE ENAME='&&NAME')AND
  4      JOB = (SELECT JOB FROM EMP WHERE ENAME = '&NAME') AND
  5*HIREDATE>(SELECT HIREDATE FROM EMP WHERE ENAME='&NAME')
SQL> /
```

Enter value for name: **BLAKE**

EMPNO	ENAME	JOB	MGR	HIREDATE	SAL	COMM	DEPTNO
8888	BIG BUCKS	MANAGER		03-MAY-88	5500		30

Now try running this query again, and notice you are not prompted for NAME, since you already declared that NAME is BLAKE the last time you executed this query. So, you must **UNDEFINE** the variable **NAME.**

```
SQL> /
```

EMPNO	ENAME	JOB	MGR	HIREDATE	SAL	COMM	DEPTNO
8888	BIG BUCKS	MANAGER		03-MAY-88	5500		30

```
SQL> UNDEFINE NAME
SQL> /
```

Enter value for name: **BLAKE**

EMPNO	ENAME	JOB	MGR	HIREDATE	SAL	COMM	DEPTNO
8888	BIG BUCKS	MANAGER		03-MAY-88	5500		30

Suppressing Prompts

Method 1:

```
SQL> SHOW SCAN
scan ON

SQL> TTITLE 'Keystone Stealth & Bombers'
Enter value for bombers: Oh No - I Got Prompted!!!


SQL> SET SCAN OFF
SQL> TTITLE 'Keystone Stealth & Bombers'
SQL> SELECT *
  2  FROM    DEPT
  3  WHERE   DEPTNO = 10;
```

```
Sat Sep 16       Keystone Stealth & Bombers       page      1

 DEPTNO DNAME          LOC
------- -------------- -------------
     10 ACCOUNTING     NEW YORK
```

Method 2:

```
SQL> SHOW DEF
define "&" (hex 26)

SQL> SET DEF ?
SQL> TTITLE 'Keystone Stealth & Bombers'
SQL> SELECT *
  2  FROM    DEPT
  3  WHERE   DEPTNO = 10;
```

```
Sat Sep 16       Keystone Stealth & Bombers       page      1

 DEPTNO DNAME          LOC
------- -------------- -------------
     10 ACCOUNTING     NEW YORK
```

(Continued)

The problem with the last two methods is you cannot use a bind variable in the "WHERE" clause.

```
SQL> SHOW DEF
define "?" (hex 3f)

SQL> SELECT *
  2  FROM    DEPT
  3* WHERE   DEPTNO = &DNO;

Bind variable "DNO" not declared.
```

Ok, let's try another approach using "SCAN".

```
SQL> SET DEF &
SQL> SET SCAN OFF

SQL> SELECT *
  2  FROM    DEPT
  3* WHERE   DEPTNO = &DNO;

Bind variable "DNO" not declared.
```

Method 3:

```
SQL> SET DEF ^
SQL> TTITLE 'Keystone & Lockstone'
SQL> SELECT *
  2  FROM    DEPT
  3  WHERE   DEPTNO = ^DNO;
Enter value for dno: 10
```

```
Sat Sep 16        Keystone & Lockstone        page        1

 DEPTNO DNAME          LOC
------- -------------- -------------
     10 ACCOUNTING     NEW YORK
```

Writing Subqueries Returning Multiple Values

Identify the most senior employees in each department.

```
SQL> SELECT  DEPTNO,  ENAME,  HIREDATE
  2  FROM    EMP
  3  WHERE  (DEPTNO,HIREDATE) IN(SELECT  DEPTNO,MIN(HIREDATE)
  4                                      FROM    EMP
  5*                                     GROUP  BY      DEPTNO);


    DEPTNO ENAME        HIREDATE
    ------ ----------   ---------
        10 CLARK        09-JUN-81
        20 SMITH        17-DEC-80
        30 ALLEN        20-FEB-81
        88 PAIGE        29-JAN-76

4 rows selected.
```

Using Set Operators In Subqueries

```
SQL> get cb307
  1  SELECT  ENAME, SAL
  2  FROM    EMP
  3  WHERE   SAL     IN(SELECT MAX(SAL) FROM EMP
  4                     UNION
  5*                    SELECT MIN(SAL) FROM EMP)
SQL> /

ENAME           SAL
----------  -------
SMITH           800
BIG BUCKS      5500

2 rows selected.
```

To verify the results:

```
SQL> SELECT  ENAME, SAL
  2  FROM    EMP
  3* ORDER   BY      SAL DESC;


ENAME           SAL
----------  -------
BIG BUCKS      5500
KING           5000
PAIGE          4400
SCOTT          3000
FORD           3000
JONES          2975
BLAKE          2850
CLARK          2450
ALLEN          1600
TURNER         1500
MILLER         1300
WARD           1250
MARTIN         1250
ADAMS          1100
JAMES           950
SMITH           800

16 rows selected.
```

Writing Correlated Subqueries Using Exists

```
SQL> SELECT *
  2  FROM    DEPT  /*  ID All Departments That Have Emps */
  3  WHERE   EXISTS (SELECT 'DEPTS WITH EMPS'
  4                  FROM    EMP
  5*                 WHERE   DEPT.DEPTNO = EMP.DEPTNO);

 DEPTNO DNAME          LOC
------- -------------- -------------
     10 ACCOUNTING     NEW YORK
     20 RESEARCH       DALLAS
     30 SALES          CHICAGO

3 rows selected.
```

Hello McFly. This is a CORRELATED query, which can be very slow. There are MUCH BETTER methods.

```
SQL> get cb314
  1  SELECT DEPTNO FROM DEPT
  2  INTERSECT
  3* SELECT DEPTNO FROM EMP
SQL> /

 DEPTNO
-------
     10
     20
     30
3 rows selected.
```

```
SQL> SELECT DISTINCT EMP.DEPTNO, LOC
  2  FROM    EMP,      DEPT
  3* WHERE   EMP.DEPTNO  =  DEPT.DEPTNO;

 DEPTNO LOC
------- -------------
     10 NEW YORK
     20 DALLAS
     30 CHICAGO

3 rows selected.
```

Writing Correlated Subqueries Using Not Exists

Identify all empty departments.

```
SQL> SELECT *
  2  FROM    DEPT
  3  WHERE   NOT EXISTS (SELECT 'I LOVE IOUW'
  4                      FROM    EMP
  5*                     WHERE   DEPT.DEPTNO = EMP.DEPTNO);

DEPTNO  DNAME          LOC
------- -------------- -------------
     40 OPERATIONS     BOSTON
     99 MIS            MAUI
2 rows selected.
```

I know McFly, there are better, and faster methods.
```
SQL> SELECT DEPTNO FROM DEPT
  2  MINUS
  3* SELECT DEPTNO FROM EMP;
 DEPTNO
-------
     40
     99
2 rows selected.

SQL> SELECT DISTINCT DEPTNO FROM EMP;
 DEPTNO
-------
     10
     20
     30
     88
4 rows selected.
SQL> SELECT DISTINCT DEPTNO FROM DEPT;
 DEPTNO
-------
     10
     20
     30
     40
     99
5 rows selected.
```

Another Way To Write Correlated Subqueries

Prompt for and identify the top "N" monthly salaried
employees.

```
SQL> SELECT ENAME, SAL
  2  FROM    EMP
  3  WHERE   &N > (SELECT COUNT(*)
  4                FROM   EMP S
  5                WHERE  EMP.SAL < S.SAL)
  6* ORDER   BY    SAL    DESC;

Enter value for n: 3

ENAME           SAL
---------- -------
BIG BUCKS      5500
KING           5000
PAIGE          4400

3 rows selected.
```

Or, if you want to prompt for and identify the lowest "N"
monthly salaried employees, you can solve it this way:

```
SQL> SELECT ENAME, SAL
  2  FROM    EMP
  3  WHERE   &N > (SELECT COUNT(*)
  4                FROM   EMP S
  5                WHERE  EMP.SAL > S.SAL)
  6* ORDER BY    SAL DESC;

Enter value for n: 3
ENAME           SAL
---------- -------
ADAMS          1100
JAMES           950
SMITH           800

3 rows selected.
```

Identify Employees Earning Above Average Monthly Salaries In Their Department

```
SQL> get cb397
  1  BREAK ON DEPTNO SKIP 1
  2  COL    SAL HEADING "Monthly|Salary" FORMAT $99,999
  3  SET    SPACE  5
  4  SELECT DEPTNO, SAL, ENAME
  5  FROM   EMP X
  6  WHERE  X.SAL > (SELECT AVG(SAL)
  7                  FROM   EMP
  8                  WHERE  X.DEPTNO = EMP.DEPTNO)
  9  ORDER  BY        DEPTNO;
 10  CLEAR  BREAKS
 11* SET    SPACE     1
SQL> @cb397
```

```
               Monthly
DEPTNO          Salary    ENAME
-------        --------   ----------
    10         $5,000     KING

    20         $2,975     JONES
               $3,000     SCOTT
               $3,000     FORD

    30         $2,850     CAROLE
               $4,400     DEBRA
               $5,500     PAIGE
```

```
7 rows selected.
```

```
Don't get too excited about this query.  The inner query
fires once for every row in the outer query.  If the EMP
table has 100,000 rows, the inner query fires 100,000 times.
You have enough time to play nine holes at your nearest golf
course.
```

> *Do you know why 6 is afraid of 7? Because 7 8 9 .*

Avoiding Error ORA-01427

```
SQL> SELECT *
  2  FROM    EMP
  3  WHERE   JOB = (SELECT JOB
  4                 FROM    EMP
  5*                WHERE   ENAME IN('KING', 'BLAKE'));
```

ERROR:
ORA-01427: single-row subquery returns more than one row

no rows selected

I guess it's all **IN** the way you write it!


```
SQL> get cb318
  1  SELECT *
  2  FROM    EMP
  3  WHERE   JOB IN (SELECT JOB
  4                  FROM    EMP
  5*                 WHERE   ENAME IN('KING', 'BLAKE'))
SQL> /
```

EMPNO	ENAME	JOB	MGR	HIREDATE	SAL	COMM	DEPTNO
7566	JONES	MANAGER	7839	02-APR-81	2975		20
8888	BIG BUCKS	MANAGER		03-MAY-88	5500		30
7782	CLARK	MANAGER	7839	09-JUN-81	2450		10
7698	BLAKE	MANAGER	7839	01-MAY-81	2850		30
7839	KING	PRESIDENT		17-NOV-81	5000		10

5 rows selected.

CHAPTER

10 *Main Course Steak*
(Du Bifteck)
Or
SQL To Generate SQL

Disabling All Constraints

But first, let's add some constraints.

```
SQL> ALTER TABLE DEPT
  2        ADD    CONSTRAINT  PK_DEPT_DEPTNO
  3        PRIMARY KEY(DEPTNO)  -- 2K Because Very Small
  4        USING INDEX
  5        TABLESPACE USER_INDEX
  6        STORAGE(INITIAL 2K   NEXT 2K);
```

Table altered.

```
SQL> ALTER TABLE EMP
  2        ADD    CONSTRAINT FK_EMP_DEPTNO
  3        FOREIGN KEY(DEPTNO)
  4*       REFERENCES DEPT(DEPTNO)
SQL> /
```

Table altered.

```
SQL> ALTER TABLE EMP
  2        ADD    CONSTRAINT PK_EMP_EMPNO
  3        PRIMARY KEY(EMPNO)  -- 2K Because Very Small
  4        USING   INDEX
  5        TABLESPACE USER_DATA
  6        STORAGE(INITIAL 2K      NEXT 2K);
```

Table altered.

```
SQL> ALTER TABLE EMP
  2        ADD    CONSTRAINT FK_EMP_MGR
  3        FOREIGN KEY(MGR)
  4*       REFERENCES EMP(EMPNO)
SQL> /
```

Table altered.

(Continued)

```
SQL> get cb380
  1  SET ECHO      OFF
  2  SET HEADING   OFF
  3  SET FEEDBACK OFF
  4  SET PAGESIZE 60
  5  SPOOL disable.sql
  6  select 'ALTER TABLE ' || table_name ||
  7        ' DISABLE CONSTRAINT ' || constraint_name || ';'
  8  from   USER_CONSTRAINTS
  9  where table_name in('DEPT','EMP') -- Limit And FK's 1st
 10  order   by   CONSTRAINT_TYPE DESC;
 11  SPOOL        OFF
 12  SET ECHO     ON
 13  SET HEADING  ON
 14  SET FEEDBACK ON
 15* START disable
```

ALTER TABLE EMP DISABLE CONSTRAINT UN_EMP_ENAME;
ALTER TABLE EMP DISABLE CONSTRAINT FK_EMP_DEPTNO;
ALTER TABLE EMP DISABLE CONSTRAINT FK_EMP_MGR;
ALTER TABLE DEPT DISABLE CONSTRAINT PK_DEPT_DEPTNO;
ALTER TABLE EMP DISABLE CONSTRAINT PK_EMP_EMPNO;
ALTER TABLE EMP DISABLE CONSTRAINT SYS_C007138;
ALTER TABLE EMP DISABLE CONSTRAINT CK_EMP_SAL;
SQL> SET HEADING   ON
SQL> SET FEEDBACK ON
SQL> START disable
SQL> ALTER TABLE EMP DISABLE CONSTRAINT UN_EMP_ENAME;
Table altered.
*SQL> ALTER TABLE EMP DISABLE CONSTRAINT **FK_EMP_DEPTNO**;*
Table altered.
*SQL> ALTER TABLE EMP DISABLE CONSTRAINT **FK_EMP_MGR**;*
Table altered.
*SQL> ALTER TABLE DEPT DISABLE CONSTRAINT **PK_DEPT_DEPTNO**;*
Table altered.
*SQL> ALTER TABLE EMP DISABLE CONSTRAINT **PK_EMP_EMPNO**;*
Table altered.
SQL> ALTER TABLE EMP DISABLE CONSTRAINT SYS_C007138;
Table altered.
SQL> ALTER TABLE EMP DISABLE CONSTRAINT CK_EMP_SAL;
Table altered.

Enabling All Constraints

```
SQL> SET ECHO      OFF
  2  SET HEADING   OFF
  3  SET FEEDBACK OFF
  4  SET PAGESIZE 60
  5  SPOOL enable.sql
  6  select 'ALTER TABLE ' || table_name ||
  7         ' ENABLE CONSTRAINT ' || constraint_name || ';'
  8  from    USER_CONSTRAINTS
  9  where table_name in('DEPT','EMP')  --Limit And PK's 1st
 10  order   by CONSTRAINT_TYPE;
 11  SPOOL        OFF
 12  SET ECHO     ON
 13  SET HEADING  ON
 14  SET FEEDBACK ON
 15* START enable
SQL> @cb379
ALTER TABLE EMP ENABLE CONSTRAINT SYS_C007138;
ALTER TABLE EMP ENABLE CONSTRAINT CK_EMP_SAL;
ALTER TABLE DEPT ENABLE CONSTRAINT PK_DEPT_DEPTNO;
ALTER TABLE EMP ENABLE CONSTRAINT PK_EMP_EMPNO;
ALTER TABLE EMP ENABLE CONSTRAINT FK_EMP_DEPTNO;
ALTER TABLE EMP ENABLE CONSTRAINT FK_EMP_MGR;
ALTER TABLE EMP ENABLE CONSTRAINT UN_EMP_ENAME;
SQL> SET HEADING  ON
SQL> SET FEEDBACK ON
SQL> START enable
SQL> ALTER TABLE EMP ENABLE CONSTRAINT SYS_C007138;
Table altered.
SQL> ALTER TABLE EMP ENABLE CONSTRAINT CK_EMP_SAL;
Table altered.
SQL> ALTER TABLE DEPT ENABLE CONSTRAINT PK_DEPT_DEPTNO;
Table altered.
SQL> ALTER TABLE EMP ENABLE CONSTRAINT PK_EMP_EMPNO;
Table altered.
SQL> ALTER TABLE EMP ENABLE CONSTRAINT FK_EMP_DEPTNO;
Table altered.
SQL> ALTER TABLE EMP ENABLE CONSTRAINT FK_EMP_MGR;
Table altered.
SQL> ALTER TABLE EMP ENABLE CONSTRAINT UN_EMP_ENAME;
Table altered.
```

Automating Table Name & Number Of Rows

```
SQL> get cb370
  1   SET ECHO      OFF
  2   SET HEADING   OFF
  3   SET FEEDBACK  OFF
  4   SET TERMOUT   OFF
  5   SET PAGESIZE 60
  6   SPOOL rows_per_table.sql
  7   select 'SELECT '||''''||table_name||''''||
         ',count(*) from '
  8          || table_name || ';'
  9   from    user_tables
 10   order   by table_name;
 11   SPOOL         OFF
 12   SET TERMOUT   ON
 13   START rows_per_table
 14   SET HEADING   ON
 15   SET FEEDBACK  ON
 16*  SET ECHO      ON
SQL>@cb370
SQL> SET ECHO      OFF


DEPT           5

EMP           16

PARTS         21

PLAN_TABLE       2

SINGLE_FEMALES      3

SINGLE_MALES       3
```

Automating Backup Of Small Tables With Inserts

```
SQL> get cb371
  1  SET ECHO      OFF
  2  SET LINESIZE 90
  3  SET HEADING  OFF
  4  SET FEEDBACK OFF
  5  SET TERMOUT  OFF
  6  SET PAGESIZE 60
  7  SPOOL insert_into_emp.sql
  8  select 'INSERT INTO EMP VALUES(' ||
  9         empno || ','              ||
 10         '''' || ename || ''''     || ',' ||
 11  '''' ||job ||''''||','||decode(mgr,null,'NULL',mgr)||
 12        ',' || '''' || hiredate || '''' || ',' ||
 13  sal || ',' || decode(comm,null,'NULL',comm) || ',' ||
 14  deptno            || ');'
 15  from    emp
 16  order   by    empno;
 17  SPOOL         OFF
 18  SET HEADING  ON
 19  SET FEEDBACK ON
 20  SET PAGESIZE 24
 21  SET LINESIZE 80
 22* SET ECHO      ON

SQL> @cb371

SQL> !more insert_into_emp.sql
```

```
INSERT INTO EMP VALUES(7369,'SMITH','CLERK',7902,'17-DEC-80',800,NULL,20);
INSERT INTO EMP VALUES(7499,'ALLEN','SALESMAN',7698,'20-FEB-81',1600,300,30);
INSERT INTO EMP VALUES(7521,'WARD','SALESMAN',7698,'22-FEB-81',1250,500,30);
INSERT INTO EMP VALUES(7566,'JONES','MANAGER',7839,'02-APR-81',2975,NULL,20);
INSERT INTO EMP VALUES(7654,'MARTIN','SALESMAN',7698,'28-SEP-81',1250,1400,30);
INSERT INTO EMP VALUES(7698,'BLAKE','MANAGER',7839,'01-MAY-81',2850,NULL,30);
INSERT INTO EMP VALUES(7782,'CLARK','MANAGER',7839,'09-JUN-81',2450,NULL,10);
INSERT INTO EMP VALUES(7788,'SCOTT','ANALYST',7566,'09-DEC-82',3000,NULL,20);
INSERT INTO EMP VALUES(7839,'KING','PRESIDENT',NULL,'17-NOV-81',5000,NULL,10);
INSERT INTO EMP VALUES(7844,'TURNER','SALESMAN',7698,'08-SEP-81',1500,0,30);
INSERT INTO EMP VALUES(7876,'ADAMS','CLERK',7788,'12-JAN-83',1100,NULL,20);
INSERT INTO EMP VALUES(7900,'JAMES','CLERK',7698,'03-DEC-81',950,NULL,30);
INSERT INTO EMP VALUES(7902,'FORD','ANALYST',7566,'03-DEC-81',3000,NULL,20);
INSERT INTO EMP VALUES(7934,'MILLER','CLERK',7782,'23-JAN-82',1300,NULL,10);
INSERT INTO EMP VALUES(8888,'BIG BUCKS','MANAGER',7566,'03-MAY-88',5500,NULL,30);
INSERT INTO EMP VALUES(8889,'PAIGE','ANALYST',7566,'29-JAN-76',4400,NULL,30);
```

Automating SQL*ReportWriter Reports By Department

```
SQL> get cb372
  1  REM Produces Separate Disk File Reports For Each Department
  2  REM Found In The Department Table At The End Of A Day At The
  3  REM Request Of A Customer In Atlanta, Georgia
  4  REM A Real "PEACH" Of A Report
  5  REM i.e. Say We Have Departments 10 and 20 At The End Of Today
  6  REM This Script Would Create A File With The Following Two
  7  REM SQL*ReportWriter V1.1 Commands:
  8  REM runrep daily student15/student15 no dno=10 destype=file desname=f10
  9  REM runrep daily student15/student15 no dno=20 destype=file desname=f20
 10  REM The "daily" Report Prompts For A Department Number Using
 11  REM A "Bind" Parameter
 12  SET ECHO     OFF
 13  SET HEADING  OFF
 14  SET FEEDBACK OFF
 15  SPOOL srw_daily.lis
 16  select 'runrep daily student15/student15 no ' ||
 17       'dno=' || deptno ||
 18       ' destype=file desname=f' || deptno
 19  from     dept
 20  order   by   deptno;
 21  SPOOL        OFF
 22  SET HEADING  ON
 23  SET FEEDBACK ON
 24  SET ECHO     ON
 25  host chmod 777 srw_daily.lis
 26  host srw_daily.lis
 27* exit

SQL> @cb372

runrep daily student15/student15 no dno=10 destype=file desname=f10
runrep daily student15/student15 no dno=20 destype=file desname=f20
runrep daily student15/student15 no dno=30 destype=file desname=f30
runrep daily student15/student15 no dno=40 destype=file desname=f40
runrep daily student15/student15 no dno=99 destype=file desname=f99

SQL> host chmod 777 srw_daily.lis
SQL> host srw_daily.lis
SQL> exit
Disconnected from Oracle7 Server Release 7.1.3.0.0 - Production Release
With the distributed and parallel query options
PL/SQL Release 2.1.3.0.0 - Production
>
```

A famous female jazz singer in Hollywood, Ella ??, is getting a divorce after 47 years of marriage. What has some folks upset is the fact she is going to re-marry a 17 year old boy by the name of Darth Vader. So now her new name will be ELLA VADER.

CHAPTER

11 *In Closing*

Oh Why, Oh Why Does My Query Run Twice ?

```
SQL> SELECT *
  2  FROM   DEPT;

 DEPTNO DNAME          LOC
 ------- -------------- -------------
     10 ACCOUNTING     NEW YORK
     20 RESEARCH       DALLAS
     30 SALES          CHICAGO
     40 OPERATIONS     BOSTON

SQL> save cb500
Created file cb500

SQL> edit cb500
SELECT *
FROM   DEPT
/
```

Notice, after saving a file from the "SQL>" prompt, Oracle places a forward slash on the last line. If you add a semicolon after "DEPT", the SQL statement executes TWICE !!

```
SELECT *
FROM   DEPT;
/

SQL> @cb500

  DEPTNO DNAME          LOC
 ------- -------------- -------------
     10 ACCOUNTING     NEW YORK
     20 RESEARCH       DALLAS
     30 SALES          CHICAGO
     40 OPERATIONS     BOSTON

  DEPTNO DNAME          LOC
 ------- -------------- -------------
     10 ACCOUNTING     NEW YORK
     20 RESEARCH       DALLAS
     30 SALES          CHICAGO
     40 OPERATIONS     BOSTON
```

Oh One Last Report, Oh Baby One Last Report

```
SQL> get cb501
  1  set space    8
  2  set pagesize 32
  3  col dte format a10 NEW_VALUE better_date noprint
  4  col sal format $99,999 heading 'Monthly|Salary'
  5  ttitle left 'Date: ' better_date -
  6         center 'Payroll By department' -
  7         skip 3
  8  btitle 'For Your Eyes Only'
  9  break on deptno skip 1 on report
 10  compute sum avg of sal on deptno report
 11  set feedback off
 12  SELECT deptno, ename, sal, job,
 13         to_char(sysdate,'MM/DD/YYYY') dte
 14  FROM   emp
 15  WHERE  deptno in(10,20)
 16  ORDER  by deptno, sal desc;
 17  set space    1
 18  set pagesize 24
 19  ttitle off
 20  btitle off
 21  clear breaks
 22* clear computes

SQL> @cb501


Date: 10/10/1995                 Payroll By Department


DEPTNO       ENAME               Salary      JOB
-------      ----------         --------    ---------
     10      KING               $5,000      PRESIDENT
             CLARK              $2,450      MANAGER
             MILLER             $1,300      CLERK
*******                         --------
avg                             $2,917
sum                             $8,750


     20      SCOTT              $3,000      ANALYST
             FORD               $3,000      ANALYST
             JONES              $2,975      MANAGER
             ADAMS              $1,100      CLERK
             SMITH                $800      CLERK
*******                         --------
avg                             $2,175
sum                             $10,875


                                --------
avg                             $2,453
sum                             $19,625



                       For Your Eyes Only
```

On A Big Table You Can Query Forever

```
SQL> SELECT TABLE_NAME
  2* FROM    DICTIONARY;


^C
FROM    DICTIONARY
                  *
ERROR at line 2:
ORA-01013: user requested cancel of current operation
```

On most platforms, a control "C" aborts a long running query.

On NT platforms, click on "File" and then click on "Cancel".

Displaying The Time

Use the function TO_CHAR on the pseudo column SYSDATE to
display the current time on the terminal. The second
argument in the function TO_CHAR supplies the format. Hours
are shown using HH, minutes MI, and seconds SS.

SQL> SELECT TO_CHAR(SYSDATE,'HH:MI:SS') TIME
  2 FROM   DUAL;

TIME

08:12:43

You can also include whether or not the time is in the
morning or evening by using the format mask AM or PM.

SQL> SELECT TO_CHAR(SYSDATE,'HH:MI:SS **PM**') TIME
  2 FROM   DUAL;

TIME
----
*08:14:24 **PM***

SQL> SELECT TO_CHAR(SYSDATE,'HH:MI:SS **AM**') TIME
  2 FROM   DUAL;

TIME
----
*08:14:35 **PM***

Or, use the SET TIME ON command to display the current time
to the left of the SQL prompt. The time changes each time
you depress the enter or return key.

SQL> SHOW TIME
time OFF

SQL> SET TIME ON
20:46:44 SQL>
20:47:00 SQL>

Display the SID Or Database Name In The SQL Prompt

My students frequently ask how to display their Oracle SID in the SQL prompt. First of all, most Oracle database names and the system identifier are the same. If they are not the same, this example does not work. The name of the database is stored in the dynamic performance view called V$DATABASE in the NAME column. In this example, the name of the database is ORACLE.

```
SQL> SELECT NAME
  2  FROM    V$DATABASE;

NAME
------
ORACLE
```

Next, use the DEFINE command to define a variable that is used in the SET SQLPROMPT command. This example defines a variable named "X". To display the current setting of the environmental variable SQLPROMPT, use the SHOW SQLPROMPT command. Then, just use the variable in the SET command using the ampersand in front of the variable. The ampersand sucks in the current value of the variable, if it is defined. In this example, the &X sucks in the value of ORACLE.

```
SQL> DEF X="ORACLE>"
SQL> SET SQLPROMPT &X
ORACLE>
```

```
ORACLE>SHOW SQLPROMPT
sqlprompt "ORACLE>"
```

For those of you with a very sick sense of humor, try this command on a very close friend:
```
SQL> SET SQLPROMPT "C:\>"
C:\>
```

Determine The Average Row Length Of A Table

The easiest method to display the average row length of a table is using the ANALYZE TABLE command, and writing a query observing the contents of the AVG_ROW_LEN column in the view USER_TABLES. The average row length of the AUTO_PARTS table is 22 bytes. Before the advent of the ANALYZE TABLE command, you had to use a combination of the functions AVG and VSIZE. Notice the accuracy of both. Row overhead of 3 bytes + 3 bytes column overhead + 16.3 = 22.3.

```
SQL> DESC AUTO_PARTS
 Name                                 Null?    Type
 ----------------------------------   --------  ----
 PARTNO                               NOT NULL NUMBER(7)
 PNAME                                         VARCHAR2(15)
 PCOST                                         NUMBER(7,2)


SQL> SELECT *
  2  FROM    AUTO_PARTS;
PARTNO PNAME               PCOST
------ --------------      ------
     1 OFFY ENGINE         43000
300000 360 SPRINT          18000
700000 OUTLAW ENGINE       22000
SQL> ANALYZE TABLE AUTO_PARTS COMPUTE STATISTICS;
Table analyzed.


SQL> SELECT AVG_ROW_LEN
  2  FROM    USER_TABLES
  3  WHERE   TABLE_NAME = UPPER('&TN');
Enter value for tn: AUTO_PARTS
AVG_ROW_LEN
-----------
         22


SQL> SELECT 3 ROW_OVERHEAD,
  2          3 *1 COL_OVERHEAD,
  3          AVG(VSIZE(PARTNO))+AVG(VSIZE(PNAME))+
  4          AVG(VSIZE(PCOST)) DATA_OVERHEAD
  5  FROM    AUTO_PARTS;
ROW_OVERHEAD COL_OVERHEAD DATA_OVERHEAD
------------ ------------ -------------
           3            3        16.333
```

Is Anyone Trying To Break Into My Database?

```
SQL> SELECT SUBSTR(NAME,1,30) PARAM,
  2         SUBSTR(VALUE,1,25) CURRENT_SETTING
  3  FROM   V$PARAMETER
  4  WHERE  NAME LIKE '%' || LOWER('&Parameter') || '%';

Enter value for parameter: audit_trail
PARAM                          CURRENT_SETTING
------------------------------ -------------------------
audit_trail                    DB

SQL> AUDIT CONNECT
  2        WHENEVER NOT SUCCESSFUL;
Audit succeeded.

SQL> CONNECT DEBRA/KAY
ERROR: ORA-01017: invalid username/password; logon denied
Warning: You are no longer connected to ORACLE.

SQL> CONNECT PAIGE/LARUE
ERROR: ORA-01017: invalid username/password; logon denied

SQL> CONNECT BONNIE/TOBIE
ERROR: ORA-01017: invalid username/password; logon denied

SQL> CONNECT CAROLE/THE_COW
ERROR: ORA-01017: invalid username/password; logon denied

SQL> CONNECT HARRY/THE_HORSE
ERROR: ORA-01017: invalid username/password; logon denied

➢ sqlplus system/manager

SQL> SELECT USERID  --These 5 User Names Tried To Connect
  2  FROM   SYS.AUD$;

USERID
------
DEBRA
PAIGE
BONNIE
CAROLE
HARRY
```

Database Triggers For True Value Auditing

```
SQL> CREATE TABLE AUDIT_DEPT
  2    (WHO          VARCHAR2(30),
  3     WHEN         DATE,
  4     OLD_DEPTNO NUMBER(2,0),
  5     NEW_DEPTNO NUMBER(2,0),
  6     OLD_DNAME    VARCHAR2(14),
  7     NEW_DNAME    VARCHAR2(14),
  8     OLD_LOC      VARCHAR2(14),
  9     NEW_LOC      VARCHAR2(14));
```
Table created.

```
SQL> CREATE TRIGGER ROY
  2  AFTER INSERT OR
  3         UPDATE OR
  4         DELETE
  5  ON      DEPT
  6  FOR     EACH ROW
  7  BEGIN
  8      IF INSERTING THEN
  9         INSERT into audit_dept
 10         VALUES(user,sysdate,null,:NEW.deptno,
 11               null, :NEW.dname, null, :NEW.loc);
 12      ELSIF DELETING THEN
 13         INSERT into audit_dept
 14         VALUES(user,sysdate,:OLD.deptno,null,
 15               :OLD.dname,null,:OLD.loc,null);
 16      ELSIF UPDATING THEN
 17         INSERT into audit_dept
 18         VALUES(user, sysdate,
 19               :OLD.deptno,  :NEW.deptno,
 20               :OLD.dname,   :NEW.dname,
 21               :OLD.loc,     :NEW.loc);
 22      END  IF;
 23* END;
```
Trigger created.
```
SQL> UPDATE DEPT SET LOC = 'MAUI' WHERE DEPTNO IN(10,30);
SQL> DELETE FROM DEPT WHERE DEPTNO = 40;
SQL> INSERT INTO DEPT VALUES(55,'MIS','MAUI');
SQL> SELECT COUNT(*) FROM AUDIT_DEPT;
```
COUNT(*)
```
--------
       4
```

I Don't Want To Use Oracle's Default Date Format

```
SQL> SELECT ENAME, HIREDATE   -- Note Default Format
  2  FROM    EMP
  3  WHERE   ROWNUM < 2;

ENAME      HIREDATE
---------- ---------
INDY       17-DEC-80




SQL> ALTER SESSION    -- Just For My Session
  2           SET NLS_DATE_FORMAT = 'MM/DD/YY';
Session altered.




SQL> SELECT ENAME, HIREDATE
  2  FROM    EMP
  3  WHERE   ROWNUM < 2;

ENAME      HIREDATE
---------- --------
INDY       12/17/80
```

You can also set the date format for the entire database
until the next database shutdown by entering:
(If you have been granted the "ALTER SYSTEM" privilege.)

SQL>ALTER SYSTEM SET NLS_DATE_FORMAT = 'MM/DD/YY';

Warning! Any statements that update or insert will fail if
they are not using the same format as contained in the ALTER
SYSTEM command.

To make this a permanent date format, have the DBA use
MM/DD/YY in the init.ora parameter file for the setting
nls_date_format.

Explain Plan, SQL Trace, Tkprof & Query In One Command

```
SQL> SHOW AUTOTRACE
autotrace OFF
SQL> SET AUTOTRACE ON

SQL> ALTER SESSION SET SQL_TRACE = TRUE;
Session altered.
SQL> -- Alter Session command entered to produce dump file
SQL> -- For Comparison Purposes Between AUTOTRACE & TKPROF

SQL> SET TIMING ON
SQL> SELECT *
     FROM    STATS
     WHERE   SEX = 'F';
500000 rows selected.
Elapsed:  01:13:40.44
```

Execution Plan   (Greatly formatted by Your Chef)
----
0 SELECT STATEMENT Optimizer=CHOOSE(Cost=3958 Card=500000 Bytes=23500000)
1 0 TABLE ACCESS(FULL) OF 'STATS'(Cost=3958 Card=500000 Bytes=23500000)

Statistics

```
      865  recursive calls
        5  db block gets
    59527  consistent gets
    26082  physical reads
        0  redo size
 31407128  bytes sent via SQL*Net to client
   367035  bytes received via SQL*Net from client
    33336  SQL*Net roundtrips to/from client
        0  sorts (memory)
        0  sorts (disk)
   500000  rows processed
```

SQL Trace/tkprof Output

Call	count	cpu	elapsed	disk	query	current	rows
Parse	1	0.61	0.65	7	120	0	0
Execute	1	0.61	0.01	0	0	0	0
Fetch	33334	263.75	272.16	26075	59407	2	500000
------	-----	------	------	-----	-----	-	------
total	33336	264.37	272.82	26082	59527	2	500000

Explain Plan Or How Oracle Will Execute A SQL Statement

First, you must have a table Oracle can insert its plan tree for a particular SQL statement. You can either create the table manually, or use the utility script utlxplan.sql.

```
SQL> @C:\ORANT\RDBMS73\ADMIN\UTLXPLAN   (NT)
SQL> @$ORACLE_HOME/rdbms/admin/utlxplan (UNIX)
```

Second, if the table(PLAN_TABLE) is not empty, the easiest way to use the EXPLAIN PLAN tool is to remove all of the rows from the table(PLAN_TABLE).

```
SQL> TRUNCATE TABLE PLAN_TABLE;   -- If Not Empty
```

Third, place the string "EXPLAIN PLAN FOR" at the front of the SQL statement and execute.

```
SQL> EXPLAIN PLAN FOR
     SELECT *
     FROM    STATS
     WHERE   SEX = 'F';
```
Explained.

Fourth, write a SQL statement that queries the PLAN_TABLE.

```
SQL> SELECT  LPAD(' ',2*(LEVEL-1)) ||
             OPERATION || ' ' ||
             OPTIONS || ' ' ||
             OBJECT_NAME || ' ' || OPTIMIZER "Query Plan",
             COST
     FROM    PLAN_TABLE
     START   WITH ID     = 0
     CONNECT BY PRIOR ID = PARENT_ID;
```

Query Plan	Cost
SELECT STATEMENT CHOOSE	**3958**
TABLE ACCESS **FULL STATS** *ANALYZED*	*3958*

Fifth, interpret the results and take any necessary actions. From the above output, Oracle would retrieve 500,000 rows from a 1,000,000 row table(STATS) using a FULL TABLE SCAN, which is fine, and no action is taken here. However, you could try creating a BITMAP index on the SEX column. The estimated cost of 3,958 is based upon estimates of MIC - **M**emory, **I**/O, and **C**pu.

Annoying Message – Input Truncated To 1 Characters

```
SQL> EDIT PLS1

BEGIN
  FOR i IN 1..10 LOOP
    dbms_output.put_line('IRL FOREVER!!!');
  END LOOP;
END;       -- No Carriage Return After The Forward Slash
/


SQL> @PLS1
Input truncated to 1 characters

PL/SQL procedure successfully completed.
```

Now, edit the SQL script file PLS1.SQL placing a carriage return after the forward slash and re-execute. Notice the message is no longer displayed.

```
SQL> ED PLS1
/
(Place a carriage return after the forward slash.)

SQL> @PLS1

PL/SQL procedure successfully completed.
```

This message is unpredictable, but one thing is for sure. Place a carriage return after the forward slash and the message disappears.

APPENDIX

A *Oracle8 New Features*

Oracle8 Rowids Are Very Different From Oracle7 Rowids

```
SQL> SELECT ENAME, ROWID     --Oracle8 Extended Rowid
  2  FROM   EMP
  3  WHERE  ENAME = 'FORD';


ENAME      ROWID
---------- ------------------
FORD       AAAC/GAACAAAAL2AAM




SQL> SELECT ENAME, ROWID ORACLE8_EXTENDED,
  2  dbms_rowid.rowid_to_restricted(rowid,1) ORACLE7_RESTRICTED
  3  FROM   EMP
  4  WHERE  ENAME = 'FORD';


ENAME           ORACLE8_EXTENDED        ORACLE7_RESTRICTED
----------      ------------------      ------------------
FORD            AAAC/GAACAAAAL2AAM      000002F6.000C.0002
```

Because all objects in Oracle8 have an object identifier,
and Oracle8 uses relative file numbers within each
tablespace, the Oracle7 restricted rowid has been changed to
an Oracle8 extended rowid. However, to convert the Oracle8
extended rowid to an Oracle7 restricted rowid, Oracle
Corporation provides a stored package DBMS_ROWID. The
example above shows the Oracle7 restricted rowid using
ROWID_TO_RESTRICTED. FORD is in block 2F6, the 13th row in
block 2F6(C = 12 and the first row is 0), and in file number
2.

Enforcing Constraints

```
SQL> ALTER TABLE EMP
  2        ADD   CONSTRAINT CK_EMP_SAL
  3        CHECK(SAL > 700);
```
Table altered.

Assume you are going to load the EMP table with 200,000 records using SQL*Loader. To speed up the loading process, disable the check constraint created above.

```
SQL> ALTER TABLE EMP
  2        DISABLE CONSTRAINT CK_EMP_SAL;
```
Table altered.

Update FORD's monthly salary to $500 to simulate a record violating the check constraint on the SAL column.

```
SQL> UPDATE EMP SET SAL = 500 WHERE ENAME = 'FORD';
```
1 row updated.

When you try to enable the check constraint with FORD's salary in violation, you receive the following error.

```
SQL> ALTER TABLE EMP
  2        ENABLE CONSTRAINT CK_EMP_SAL;
```
ALTER TABLE EMP
*
ERROR at line 1:
ORA-02293: cannot validate (SYSTEM.CK_EMP_SAL) - check constraint violated

But, I must attend my daughter's soccer game now. I'll fix FORD tomorrow. Further violations are not permitted.

```
SQL> ALTER TABLE EMP
  2        ENFORCE CONSTRAINT CK_EMP_SAL;
```
Table altered.

```
SQL> UPDATE EMP
  2  SET    SAL = 200
  3  WHERE  ENAME = 'FORD';
```
UPDATE EMP
*   **
ERROR at line 1:
ORA-02290: check constraint (SYSTEM.CK_EMP_SAL) violated

Oracle8 Range Partitions

If you have Oracle8 and are using the Partitioning Option, you can create partitioned tables and partitioned indexes. The idea is to "DIVIDE AND CONQUER" very large tables and indexes. If a table partiton has a problem, applications and users can still query the remaining table partitions. The following example shows the RACING_PARTS table with three partitions, and each partition is in a separate tablespace.

```
SQL> CREATE TABLE RACING_PARTS
  2          (part_num          NUMBER(7,0),
  3           part_name         VARCHAR2(20),
  4           part_cost         NUMBER(8,2))
  5   PARTITION BY RANGE(part_num)
  6     (PARTITION rp250k VALUES LESS THAN (250001)
  7              TABLESPACE PARTS1,
  8      PARTITION rp500k VALUES LESS THAN (500001)
  9              TABLESPACE PARTS2,
 10      PARTITION rp1mil VALUES LESS THAN (1000001)
 11*             TABLESPACE PARTS3);
Table created.

SQL> INSERT INTO RACING_PARTS
  2          VALUES(555222,'FRONT WING',335.78);
1 row created.
```

You can specify the partition for Oracle to search in a query. This is not required, but can speed up the partition pruning process.

```
SQL> SELECT *
  2   FROM    RACING_PARTS PARTITION (RP1MIL) X
  3*  WHERE   X.PART_NUM < 600000;
```

PART_NUM	PART_NAME	PART_COST
555222	FRONT WING	335.78

Look Ma No Joins! Or Using Oracle8 Object Tables

```
SQL> CREATE  TYPE department_data AS OBJECT(
  2          deptno      NUMBER(7,0),    -- User
  3          dname       VARCHAR2(20),   -- Defined
  4*         town        VARCHAR2(20));  -- Data Type
Type created.

SQL> CREATE TABLE DEPARTMENTS_OBJECT_TABLE
  2          OF DEPARTMENT_DATA;
Table created.

SQL> INSERT INTO DEPARTMENTS_OBJECT_TABLE
  2          VALUES(department_data(222,'MIS','MAUI'));
1 row created.

SQL> SELECT REF(a)    -- Returns The Object Identifier (OID)
  2   FROM    DEPARTMENTS_OBJECT_TABLE a
  3   WHERE   DEPTNO = 222;
REF(A)
--------------------------------------------------------------------------------
0000280209217B274AC83C11D3AEE4005004945A0E217B2749C83C11D3AEE4005004945A0E00800B610000

SQL> CREATE TABLE           EMPLOYEES
  2 (empno NUMBER(7,0),lname VARCHAR2(15),msalary NUMBER(7,2),
  3          deptno_oid REF department_data SCOPE IS
  4                  DEPARTMENTS_OBJECT_TABLE);
Table created.

SQL> BEGIN
  2    FOR i IN 1..10 LOOP
  3        INSERT into employees
  4        SELECT i, 'Emp# ' || i,i*900, REF(d)
  5        FROM    departments_object_table d
  6        WHERE   d.deptno = 222;
  7    END   LOOP;
  8* END;

SQL> SELECT lname, msalary, DEREF(deptno_oid)
  2   FROM    employees  WHERE empno = 1;
LNAME               MSALARY
--------------- ---------
DEREF(DEPTNO_OID)(DEPTNO, DNAME, TOWN)
--------------------------------------------
Emp# 1                      900
DEPARTMENT_DATA(222, 'MIS', 'MAUI')
```

Nested Tables – So Much For E.F. Codd's Normalization!

```
SQL> CREATE TYPE employees_in_dept AS OBJECT
  2         (empno           NUMBER(7,0),
  3          lname           VARCHAR2(15),
  4*         msalary         NUMBER(7,2));
Type created.

SQL> CREATE TYPE nested_employees
             AS TABLE OF employees_in_dept;
Type created.

SQL> CREATE TYPE dept_data AS OBJECT
  2         (deptno          NUMBER(3,0),
  3          dname           VARCHAR2(15),
  4          town            VARCHAR2(15),
  5*         emps            NESTED_EMPLOYEES);
Type created.

SQL> CREATE TABLE DEPTS_NESTED OF dept_data
  2         OIDINDEX oid_depts_nested TABLESPACE indx
  3         NESTED TABLE emps
  4*         STORE AS empsv8;
Table created.

SQL> INSERT INTO depts_nested
  2  VALUES(222,'MIS','MAUI', nested_employees(
  3         employees_in_dept(1,'CASSIDY',8000),
  4*         employees_in_dept(2,'PERRY',3000)));
1 row created.

SQL> SELECT *
  2  FROM   DEPTS_NESTED;

  DEPTNO DNAME               TOWN
-------- --------------- ---------------
EMPS(EMPNO, LNAME, MSALARY)
------------------------------------------------------------
-------------------------------------------
     222 MIS               MAUI
NESTED_EMPLOYEES(EMPLOYEES_IN_DEPT(1, 'CASSIDY', 8000.00),
EMPLOYEES_IN_DEPT(2, 'PERRY', 3000.00))
```

Reverse Key Indexes

If you have a multiple cpu machine and numeric primary key columns, and you want to try another type of index and observe if queries run faster, you might try using reverse key indexes. A normal btree index could have the following key values in a leaf block: 1234, 1235, 1236, 1237, etc. Using a btree reverse key index, the key values are spread out in different leaf blocks. The reverse key value of 1234 becomes 4321 and is stored in a leaf block starting with say four thousand instead of a leaf block starting with one thousand. 1235 becomes 5321, 1236 becomes 6321, and 1237 becomes 7321.

The following example creates a btree reverse key index on the SAL column of the EMP table.

```
SQL> CREATE INDEX REVERSE_BTREE_ON_EMP_SAL
  2         ON EMP(SAL)
  3         REVERSE;
Index created.
```

You can change a normal btree index to a reverse key btree index using the ALTER command, as the following example illustrates.

```
SQL> CREATE INDEX INDX_EMP_COMM
  2         ON EMP(COMM)
  3*        TABLESPACE INDX;
Index created.

SQL> ALTER INDEX INDX_EMP_COMM
  2         REBUILD
  3         REVERSE;
Index altered.
```

Parallel DML (PDML)

In Oracle7 you can write PARALLEL queries using the PARALLEL hint. In Oracle8, you can write parallel INSERTs, UPDATEs, and DELETEs. For a 14 row table the use of this feature is absurd. However, for a 100 million row table, this feature can execute very quickly, particularly if you have multiple cpu's.

```
SQL> ALTER SESSION        -- Enable This First
  2         ENABLE
  3         PARALLEL DML;
Session altered.
```

```
SQL> UPDATE /*+ PARALLEL(EMP,4)  */    EMP
  2  SET     SAL = SAL + 100;
14 rows updated.
```

Two Oracle Date Default Masks

Without using the parameter nls_date_format, or the ALTER
SESSION command to set nls_date_format, or the TO_DATE
function, the default date format is DD-MON-YY. The
following query shows the Oracle default date format.

```
SQL> SELECT ENAME,
  2          HIREDATE
  3  FROM    EMP
  4  WHERE   ENAME = 'FORD';
ENAME       HIREDATE
----------  ---------
FORD        03-DEC-81
```

Somewhere along the line in one of the Oracle8 releases,
Oracle Corporation slipped the following in without me
noticing for quite a spell. Before this, you had to use the
function TO_DATE in the WHERE clause for this to work.

```
SQL> SELECT ENAME,
  2          HIREDATE
  3  FROM    EMP
  4* WHERE HIREDATE BETWEEN '17-NOV-1981' AND '03-DEC-1981';
ENAME       HIREDATE
----------  ---------
FORD        03-DEC-81
JAMES       03-DEC-81
KING        17-NOV-81
```

The following query is surprising. The query is executed in
the year 2000, and the actual year of the hiredate column is
1981 and not 2081. Therefore, no rows are returned.

```
SQL> SELECT TO_CHAR(SYSDATE,'MM/DD/YYYY') "Today"
  2  FROM    DUAL;
Today
----------
01/11/2000
```

```
SQL> SELECT ENAME,
  2          HIREDATE
  3  FROM    EMP
  4* WHERE   HIREDATE BETWEEN '17-NOV-81' AND '03-DEC-81';
no rows selected
```

Index Organized Tables (IOTs)

Index Organized Tables store data in a B*Tree structure, requiring much less disk space, since there is no need for a separate index structure. In the following example, any rows requiring more than 40% of the block size are stored in the overflow tablespace IOT_OVERFLOW_TS.

```
SQL> CREATE TABLE IOT1
  2       (document#   NUMBER,
  3        stringa     VARCHAR2(25),
  4        string_freq NUMBER,
  5        string_data VARCHAR2(200),
  6   CONSTRAINT pk_iot1_document#
  7        PRIMARY KEY(document#))
  8   ORGANIZATION INDEX    -- Index Organized Table
  9       TABLESPACE INDX
  9   PCTTHRESHOLD 40
 10* OVERFLOW TABLESPACE iot_overflow_ts;
Table created.

SQL> SELECT TABLE_NAME,TABLESPACE_NAME,IOT_NAME,IOT_TYPE
  2   FROM    DBA_TABLES
  3   WHERE   TABLE_NAME = 'IOT1' OR IOT_NAME = 'IOT1';
TABLE_NAME              TABLESPACE_NAME  IOT_NAME IOT_TYPE
------------------      ---------------  -------- ------------
SYS_IOT_OVER_12328      USERS            IOT1     IOT_OVERFLOW
IOT1                                              IOT

SQL> SELECT OBJECT_NAME, OBJECT_ID
  2   FROM    USER_OBJECTS
  3* WHERE   OBJECT_NAME LIKE '%IOT%';
OBJECT_NAME             OBJECT_ID
------------------      ---------
IOT1                    12328
PK_IOT1_DOCUMENT#       12330
SYS_IOT_OVER_12328      12329

SQL> SELECT INDEX_NAME, INDEX_TYPE, TABLESPACE_NAME
  2   FROM    DBA_INDEXES
  3* WHERE   TABLE_NAME = 'IOT1';

INDEX_NAME              INDEX_TYPE  TABLESPACE_NAME
------------------      ----------  ---------------
PK_IOT1_DOCUMENT#       IOT - TOP   INDX
```

APPENDIX

B *Oracle8i New Features*

Group By Cube

The GROUP BY CUBE clause produces a subtotal line for each department number in the following example. It also calculates a total for each job, and a grand total at the end of the query.

```
SQL> SELECT DEPTNO, JOB, COUNT(*)
     FROM    EMP
     GROUP BY CUBE(DEPTNO,JOB);
```

DEPTNO	JOB	COUNT(*)
10	CLERK	1
10	MANAGER	1
10	PRESIDENT	1
10		**3**
20	ANALYST	2
20	CLERK	2
20	MANAGER	1
20		**5**
30	CLERK	1
30	MANAGER	1
30	SALESMAN	4
30		**6**
	ANALYST	**2**
	CLERK	**4**
	MANAGER	**3**
	PRESIDENT	**1**
	SALESMAN	**4**
		14

18 rows selected.

Group By Rollup

The GROUP BY ROLLUP clause produces a subtotal line for each department number in the following example. It also calculates a grand total at the end of the query.

```
SQL> SELECT DEPTNO, JOB, COUNT(*)
  2  FROM    EMP
  3  GROUP   BY ROLLUP(DEPTNO, JOB);

   DEPTNO JOB        COUNT(*)
--------- --------- ---------
       10 CLERK             1
       10 MANAGER           1
       10 PRESIDENT         1
       10                   3
       20 ANALYST           2
       20 CLERK             2
       20 MANAGER           1
       20                   5
       30 CLERK             1
       30 MANAGER           1
       30 SALESMAN          4
       30                   6
                           14

13 rows selected.
```

Subqueries In The FROM Clause

One method of determining all employees who earn more than the average salary for their department is to create a view containing the department number and the average monthly salary. Then, join the EMP table to the view using the department numbers, returning employees whose EMP.SAL is greater than the VIEW's average salary for that particular department. You can also write a correlated subquery to solve this problem. Or, you can write a subquery in the FROM clause, as shown in the following example. Think of this subquery as a VIEW named V.

```
SQL> SELECT  ENAME, SAL, DEPTNO
  2  FROM    EMP E
  3  WHERE   E.SAL > (SELECT AVG(SAL)      -- Correlated
  4                   FROM    EMP          -- Subquery
  5                   WHERE   E.DEPTNO = EMP.DEPTNO);
```

ENAME	SAL	DEPTNO
ALLEN	1600	30
JONES	2975	20
BLAKE	2850	30
SCOTT	3000	20
KING	5000	10
FORD	3000	20

6 rows selected.

```
SQL> SELECT  E.ENAME, E.SAL, E.DEPTNO, V.AVGSAL
  2  FROM    EMP E, (SELECT DEPTNO, AVG(SAL) AVGSAL
  3                  FROM    EMP
  4                  GROUP  BY  DEPTNO) V
  5  WHERE   E.DEPTNO = V.DEPTNO AND
  6          E.SAL    > V.AVGSAL;
```

ENAME	SAL	DEPTNO	AVGSAL
KING	5000	10	2916.6667
JONES	2975	20	2175
SCOTT	3000	20	2175
FORD	3000	20	2175
ALLEN	1600	30	1566.6667
BLAKE	2850	30	1566.6667

6 rows selected.

TOP N Queries

Instead of writing the following very nasty correlated
subquery to identify the top salaried employees:

```
SQL> SELECT  ENAME, SAL
  2  FROM    EMP
  3  WHERE   &N > (SELECT COUNT(*)
  4                 FROM    EMP S
  5                 WHERE   EMP.SAL < S.SAL)
  6  ORDER  BY SAL DESC;
Enter value for n: 3
old    3: WHERE   &N > (SELECT COUNT(*)
new    3: WHERE   3 > (SELECT COUNT(*)

ENAME               SAL
----------  ---------
KING               5000
SCOTT              3000
FORD               3000
```

In Oracle8i you can write the following TOP N query to
identify the top salaried employees.

```
SQL> SELECT  ENAME,  SAL
  2  FROM    (SELECT ENAME, SAL
  3           FROM    EMP
  4           ORDER  BY SAL DESC)
  5* WHERE   ROWNUM < &TOP;

Enter value for top: 4
old    5: WHERE   ROWNUM < &TOP
new    5: WHERE   ROWNUM < 4

ENAME               SAL
----------  ---------
KING               5000
SCOTT              3000
FORD               3000
```

Oracle Corporation Writes Queries Used In Explain Plan

Finally, after all of these years and releases (1990 Version 6), Oracle Corporation has written two SQL scripts used to extract and interpret information from the table PLAN_TABLE after using the EXPLAIN PLAN command. The two scripts are named utlxpls.sql and utlxplp.sql. On UNIX platforms, the scripts are found in $ORACLE_HOME/rdbms/admin.

```
SQL> SET       VERIFY OFF
SQL> EXPLAIN PLAN   FOR
  2  SELECT ENAME,  SAL
  3  FROM    (SELECT ENAME, SAL
  4          FROM    EMP
  5          ORDER  BY SAL DESC)
  6* WHERE   ROWNUM < &TOP;
Enter value for top: 3
Explained.
```

```
SQL> @C:\ORACLE8I\RDBMS\ADMIN\UTLXPLS
```
Plan Table

Operation	Name	Rows	Bytes	Cost	Pstart	Pstop
SELECT STATEMENT						
COUNT STOPKEY						
VIEW						
SORT ORDER BY STOPKEY						
TABLE ACCESS FULL	EMP					

8 rows selected.

```
SQL> get old_explain
  1  COL     "Query Plan" FORMAT   A40
  2  SELECT  LPAD(' ',2*LEVEL-1) || OPERATION || ' ' ||
  3          OPTIONS || ' ' || OBJECT_NAME || ' ' ||
  4          OPTIMIZER "Query Plan", COST
  5  FROM    PLAN_TABLE
  6  START   WITH ID    = 0
  7* CONNECT BY PRIOR ID = PARENT_ID
SQL> @old_explain
```

Query Plan	COST
SELECT STATEMENT CHOOSE	3
COUNT STOPKEY	
VIEW	3
SORT ORDER BY STOPKEY	3
TABLE ACCESS FULL EMP ANALYZED	1

Creating Global Temporary Tables

```
SQL> SHOW USER
USER is "SYSTEM"

SQL> CREATE GLOBAL TEMPORARY TABLE IRL4VR
  2         (CARNO      VARCHAR2(4),
  3          DNAME      VARCHAR2(15),
  4          COWNER     varchar2(15));
Table created.

SQL> INSERT INTO IRL4VR
  2         VALUES('99','LEE WALLARD','BELINGER');
1 row created.


SQL> SELECT *
  2  FROM    IRL4VR;

CARN DNAME              COWNER
---- --------------- ---------------
99   LEE WALLARD      BELINGER


SQL> COMMIT;
Commit complete.


SQL> SELECT *
     FROM IRL4VR;
no rows selected
```

Dropping Columns From A Table

Oracle customers have been asking for this capability since 1988 and probably even earlier. Finally, you can drop a column from a table, or you can mark it unused and then drop the column.

```
SQL> ALTER TABLE DEPT ADD HEAD_COUNT NUMBER;
Table altered.
```

```
SQL> DESC DEPT
```

Name	Null?	Type
DEPTNO	NOT NULL	NUMBER(2)
DNAME		VARCHAR2(14)
LOC		VARCHAR2(13)
HEAD_COUNT		**NUMBER**

```
SQL> ALTER TABLE DEPT
  2       SET   UNUSED COLUMN HEAD_COUNT;
Table altered.
```

```
SQL> SELECT TABLE_NAME,
  2       COUNT
  3  FROM   USER_UNUSED_COL_TABS
  4* WHERE  TABLE_NAME = 'DEPT';
```

TABLE_NAME	COUNT
DEPT	1

```
SQL> DESC DEPT
```

Name	Null?	Type
DEPTNO	NOT NULL	NUMBER(2)
DNAME		VARCHAR2(14)
LOC		VARCHAR2(13)

```
SQL> ALTER TABLE DEPT
  2       DROP   UNUSED COLUMNS;
Table altered.
```

```
SQL> SELECT TABLE_NAME,
  2       COUNT
  3  FROM   USER_UNUSED_COL_TABS
  4* WHERE  TABLE_NAME = 'DEPT';
no rows selected
```

Function-Based Indexes

You can now create function-based indexes. As long as you remember to issue both ALTER SESSION commands, the Oracle optimizer may decide to use the function-based index when retrieving rows, as the following example suggests.

```
SQL> ALTER SESSION SET QUERY_REWRITE_ENABLED = TRUE;
Session altered.

SQL> ALTER SESSION SET QUERY_REWRITE_INTEGRITY = TRUSTED;
Session altered.

SQL> CREATE INDEX INDEX_FB_MANY_EMPS_TOT_SAL
  2          ON MANY_EMPS(SAL+COMM)
  3          TABLESPACE INDX;
Index created.

SQL> SELECT INDEX_NAME, INDEX_TYPE, UNIQUENESS
  2  FROM    USER_INDEXES
  3* WHERE   TABLE_NAME = UPPER('&TN');
Enter value for tn: MANY_EMPS


INDEX_NAME                       INDEX_TYPE              UNIQUENES
-------------------------------- ---------------------- ---------
INDEX_FB_MANY_EMPS_TOT_SAL FUNCTION-BASED NORMAL NONUNIQUE


SQL> EXPLAIN PLAN FOR
  2  SELECT  *
  3  FROM    MANY_EMPS  -- Oracle Can Now Use Index
  4  WHERE   SAL+COMM = 2100;
Explained.

SQL> @C:\ORACLE8I\RDBMS\ADMIN\UTLXPLS
```

```
Plan Table
--------------------------------------------------------------------------------
| Operation              | Name       | Rows | Bytes| Cost | Pstart| Pstop |
--------------------------------------------------------------------------------
| SELECT STATEMENT       |            |  1K|  26K|   2 |       |       |
|  TABLE ACCESS BY INDEX ROW|MANY_EMPS |  1K|  26K|   2 |       |       |
|   INDEX RANGE SCAN     |INDEX_FB_   |  1K|      |   1 |       |       |
--------------------------------------------------------------------------------
```

The TRIM Function

If you want to trim leading and trailing characters from a string, use the TRIM function.

```
SQL> SELECT TRIM('S' FROM 'SSSCASSISS')
  2  FROM    DUAL;

TRIM(
-----
CASSI
```

Database Triggers

You can now write database triggers that fire when a user logs on or logs off of Oracle. The following example fires whenever someone connects as the Oracle user SYSTEM. Database triggers now permit the COMMIT statement.

```
SQL> SHOW USER
USER is "SYS"

SQL> CREATE TABLE EVENT_LOG(WHO_AND_WHEN   VARCHAR2(70));
Table Created.

SQL> CREATE OR REPLACE TRIGGER track_logons
  2        AFTER LOGON ON DATABASE
  3        WHEN (user = 'SYSTEM')
  4  BEGIN
  5    INSERT INTO sys.event_log
  6      VALUES(user || ' Logged On At ' || to_char(sysdate,
  7         'MM/DD/YYYY HH:MI:SS'));
  8    COMMIT;  -- Can't Do This In Previous Versions
  9* END;
SQL> /
Trigger created.

SQL> SHOW TIME
time OFF

SQL> SET TIME ON
17:49:30 SQL> CONNECT SYSTEM/MANAGER
Connected.
17:49:41 SQL> SET TIME OFF


SQL> SELECT *
  2  FROM   SYS.EVENT_LOG;

WHO_AND_WHEN
----------------------------------------
SYSTEM Logged On At 01/12/2000 05:49:41
```

Hash Partitions

Hash partitions can be used for better load balancing, and offer a greater degree of parallelism for parallel data manipulation(PDML). Consider using hash partitions when you know range partitions would be skewed. The following example shows the table IRL_DRIVERS with 64 hash partitions.

```
SQL> CREATE TABLE IRL_DRIVERS
  2          ( driver_no        VARCHAR2(3),
  3            dname            VARCHAR2(25),
  4            first_year       DATE,
  5            first_car_type   VARCHAR2(6))
  6   PARTITION BY HASH( first_year )
  7*  PARTITIONS 64;
Table created.

SQL> INSERT INTO IRL_DRIVERS
  2   VALUES('99','LEE WALLARD','01-JAN-1945','MIDGET');
1 row created.

SQL> INSERT INTO IRL_DRIVERS
  2*  VALUES('222','RICH VOGLER','01-JAN-70','SPRINT');
1 row created.

SQL> EXPLAIN PLAN FOR
  2   SELECT  *
  3   FROM    IRL_DRIVERS;
Explained.

SQL> @C:\ORACLE8I\RDBMS\ADMIN\UTLXPLS
```

```
Plan Table
---------------------------------------------------------------------
| Operation            |  Name       | Rows | Bytes| Cost  | Pstart| Pstop |
---------------------------------------------------------------------
| SELECT STATEMENT     |             |  1K|  40K|   10 |       |       |
|  PARTITION HASH ALL  |             |    |     |      |   1 |   64 |
|   TABLE ACCESS FULL  | IRL_DRIVE   |  1K|  40K|   10 |   1 |   64 |
---------------------------------------------------------------------
```

Composite Partitions

Composite partitions are used for better load balancing across ranges. Consider using composite partitions when you know range partitions would be skewed. The following example shows a table RANGE partitioned on FIRST_YEAR and subpartitioned by HASH on FIRST_CAR_TYPE. Within each range, there are 2 hash subpartitions based upon a hash function applied to the hash partition key column FIRST_CAR_TYPE. Visualize a matrix with the year going across the top from left to right, and the car type running from the top to bottom.

```
SQL> CREATE TABLE IRL_DRIVERS_COMPOSITE
  2          PARTITION BY RANGE( first_year )
  3          SUBPARTITION BY HASH( first_car_type )
  4          SUBPARTITIONS 2
  5  (PARTITION IRL_P1 VALUES LESS THAN (TO_DATE('01-JAN-1960','DD-MON-YYYY')),
  6   PARTITION IRL_P2 VALUES LESS THAN (TO_DATE('01-JAN-1970','DD-MON-YYYY')),
  7   PARTITION IRL_P3 VALUES LESS THAN (TO_DATE('01-JAN-1980','DD-MON-YYYY')),
  8   PARTITION IRL_P4 VALUES LESS THAN (TO_DATE('01-JAN-1990','DD-MON-YYYY'))))
  9* AS SELECT * FROM IRL_DRIVERS;
Table created.
```

```
SQL> EXPLAIN PLAN FOR
  2  SELECT   *
  3  FROM     IRL_DRIVERS_COMPOSITE;
Explained.
```

```
SQL> @C:\ORACLE8I\RDBMS\ADMIN\UTLXPLS
```

Plan Table

Operation	Name	Rows	Bytes	Cost	Pstart	Pstop
SELECT STATEMENT		1	31	1		
PARTITION RANGE ALL					1	4
PARTITION HASH ALL					1	2
TABLE ACCESS FULL	IRL_DRIVE	1	31	1	1	8

Moving Nonpartitioned Tables To Another Tablespace

To defrag a table or eliminate chained rows, you normally export the table, drop the table, and import the table. You can also move a table from one tablespace to another to defrag and eliminate row chaining. The following example shows the table EMP_CHAINED_ROWS with 22 chained rows, in tablespace USERS, with one index INDX_SAL. The table is moved from tablespace USERS to DATA, and the index must be rebuilt.

```
SQL> SELECT CHAIN_CNT, TABLESPACE_NAME
  2  FROM    USER_TABLES
  3* WHERE   TABLE_NAME = 'EMP_CHAINED_ROWS';
CHAIN_CNT TABLESPACE_NAME
--------- ---------------
       22 USERS
SQL> SELECT INDEX_NAME, TABLESPACE_NAME
  2  FROM    USER_INDEXES
  3* WHERE   TABLE_NAME = 'EMP_CHAINED_ROWS';
INDEX_NAME  TABLESPACE_NAME
----------  ---------------
INDX_SAL    INDX

SQL> ALTER TABLE EMP_CHAINED_ROWS MOVE TABLESPACE DATA;
Table altered.

SQL> SELECT *
  2  FROM    EMP_CHAINED_ROWS
  3  WHERE   SAL = 5000;
FROM    EMP_CHAINED_ROWS
        *
ERROR at line 2:
ORA-01502: index 'SYSTEM.INDX_SAL' or partition of such index is
in unusable state

SQL> ALTER INDEX INDX_SAL REBUILD TABLESPACE INDX ONLINE;
Index altered.
SQL> ANALYZE TABLE EMP_CHAINED_ROWS COMPUTE STATISTICS;
Table analyzed.

SQL> SELECT CHAIN_CNT, TABLESPACE_NAME
  2  FROM    USER_TABLES
  3* WHERE   TABLE_NAME = 'EMP_CHAINED_ROWS';
CHAIN_CNT TABLESPACE_NAME
--------- ---------------
        0 DATA
```

Exporting Particular Rows Using The Query Parameter

Thanks to the new export parameter, QUERY, you can now export particular rows from a table. The following example shows an export of all employees in department number 10 from the EMP table.

C:\>exp help=yes

```
Keyword    Description (Default)        Keyword      Description (Default)
-------------------------------------------------------------------------
USERID     username/password           FULL         export entire file (N)
BUFFER     size of data buffer         OWNER        list of owner usernames
FILE       output files (EXPDAT.DMP)   TABLES       list of table names
COMPRESS   import into one extent (Y)  RECORDLENGTH length of IO record
GRANTS     export grants (Y)           INCTYPE      incremental export type
INDEXES    export indexes (Y)          RECORD       track incr. export (Y)
ROWS       export data rows (Y)        PARFILE      parameter filename
CONSTRAINTS export constraints (Y)     CONSISTENT   cross-table consistency
LOG        log file of screen output   STATISTICS   analyze objects (ESTIMATE)
DIRECT     direct path (N)             TRIGGERS     export triggers (Y)
FEEDBACK   display progress every x rows (0)
FILESIZE   maximum size of each dump file
QUERY      select clause used to export a subset of a table

The following keywords only apply to transportable tablespaces
TRANSPORT_TABLESPACE export transportable tablespace metadata (N)
TABLESPACES list of tablespaces to transport

Export terminated successfully without warnings.
```

C:\>exp query='where deptno=10' file=emp10.dmp tables=emp userid=system/manager

```
Export: Release 8.1.5.0.0 - Production on Sun Jan 23 09:55:22 2000

(c) Copyright 1999 Oracle Corporation.  All rights reserved.


Connected to: Oracle8i Enterprise Edition Release 8.1.5.0.0 - Production
With the Partitioning and Java options
PL/SQL Release 8.1.5.0.0 - Production
Export done in WE8ISO8859P1 character set and WE8ISO8859P1 NCHAR character set

About to export specified tables via Conventional Path ...
. . exporting table                            EMP          3 rows exported
Export terminated successfully without warnings.
```

Index

About the Author

Pete Cassidy has worked with Oracle Products since the spring of 1988 as a principal instructor at Oracle Corporation for nearly six years, where he was the number one USA instructor 1991-1993 with 74 perfect teaches. His peers voted him as the most helpful instructor in Oracle USA. Since August of 1993, Pete has been with Database Consultants Inc., of Dallas, Texas as a Senior Principal Instructor/Consultant. Pete has made many Oracle user group presentations including the UK, Oracle Open World, Midwest Oracle Users Group, Dallas Oracle Users Group, SCOUG, and has conducted 165 customized on-site Oracle classes as of 01-JAN-2000. He wrote the tuning portion of the Oracle DBA Chaucey Exam, and has written another book entitled *High Performance Oracle8 SQL Programming and Tuning, published by The Coriolis Group, ISBN 1-57610-213-0,* that teaches the reader how to tune SQL statements.

Pete is currently writing another cookbook, entitled "Pete Cassidy's Cookbook For Oracle8i SQL Statement Tuning", and should be available late 2000.

To Order Additional Copies of Pete Cassidy's Cookbook For Oracle SQL*Plus, call 972-307-3222 or email carolechef@aol.com.